This book is dedicated to those choice servants of the Lord who have served faithfully and wholeheartedly on church staffs and Christian school faculties over the years. Your commitment to service—many times with little recognition or compensation—has not gone unnoticed by others. It has been a continual and living illustration to me and many others of what a true servant of the Lord should be. Thank you for your genuine Christianity.

HOW TO BE A

TEAM PLAYER

AND ENJOY IT

A STUDY
IN STAFF RELATIONSHIPS

MATT WILLIAMS

AMBASSADOR INTERNATIONAL
GREENVILLE, SOUTH CAROLINA & BELFAST, NORTHERN IRELAND

www.ambassador-international.com

How To Be Team Player and Enjoy It:

A Study in Staff Relationships

ISBN: 978-1-62020-235-7
eISBN: 978-1-62020-333-0

Unless otherwise indicated, Scripture taken from the King James Version of the Holy Bible. Public Domain.

AMBASSADOR INTERNATIONAL
Emerald House
427 Wade Hampton Blvd.
Greenville, SC 29609, USA
www.ambassador-international.com

AMBASSADOR BOOKS
The Mount
2 Woodstock Link
Belfast, BT6 8DD, Northern Ireland, UK
www.ambassadormedia.co.uk

The colophon is a trademark of Ambassador

CONTENTS

FOREWORD

DR. MATT WILLIAMS IS A choice servant of the Lord, with special wisdom about the practical side of everyday ministry. Matt is a humble, unassuming person with a warm servant's heart. He and his wife Donna have a special love for young people, and have seen their five grown children follow their steps into service for Christ. My wife and I have benefited from their kind hospitality on various occasions; they have always made us feel at home. Matt is a forty-plus-year veteran of local church and Christian college service. He has assisted numerous ministries with staff training and has organized high school leadership conferences throughout the United States for many years.

My heart resonates with Matt's in our common interest in the practical side of local church ministry. For years I have had Bob Jones University's freshmen ministerial students read *Biblical Leadership*, co-authored by Ken Collier and Matt, as the first book they read during the school year. Then I require our exiting senior ministerial students to read as their last book, just before they graduate, *How to Be a Team Player and Enjoy It!* The combination of these books is unbeatable for down-to-earth godly and practical wisdom.

I highly commend this revised edition of *Teamplayer* to all those involved in ministry, whether full-time or volunteer. I encourage pastors to encourage their staff members to read through *Teamplayer* and discuss its vital principles. The new "Further Reflections" from

Matt's ministry friends bring additional value to the book.

May God enrich your ministry through the wisdom God has given to Matt to assist in building up Christ's church in this day!

Bruce McAllister

Director of Ministerial Training and Outreach

Bob Jones University

Greenville, South Carolina

ACKNOWLEDGMENTS

- To my wife, Donna, for being such a godly helpmeet and support to me in the ministry for over forty years.

- To my colaborer, Amy Miller, for all your input and help in editing this revised edition. I also want to thank my friend Craig Krueger for his invaluable editing in the first edition.

- To the wonderful staff of Tri-City Ministries, for all your encouragement and godly example over the many years I served with you on the pastoral staff.

- To the special servants of the Lord at Northland Baptist Bible College/Northland International University, who were such an encouragement to me in the years I was privileged to serve there.

- To my friend Ron Raymer for the illustrations.

- To my ministry friends who wrote their Further Reflections at the conclusion of each chapter.

- To my five children—Kevin, Valarie, Kari, Joy, and Chad—for their continual encouragement and support over the years. I love you!

- And now with this new edition, to my two daughters-in-law, Holly and McKenna: what wonderful additions to our family!

- Three sons-in-law, Adam, Tim, and Joel: what godly husbands, fathers, and Christian leaders you are. Thank you!

- As of this printing, sixteen grandchildren—what a blessing you are!

PREPARATION OF
THE PERSON

CHAPTER I

THE CALL TO SERVANTHOOD

And whosoever will be chief among you, let him be your servant:
Even as the Son of man came not to be ministered unto, but to minister,
and to give his life a ransom for many.

Matthew 20:27–28

But Jesus called them to him, and saith unto them,
"Ye know that they which are accounted to rule over the Gentiles exercise
lordship over them;
and their great ones exercise authority upon them.
But so shall it not be among you: but whosoever will be great among you,
shall be your minister:
And whosoever of you will be the chiefest, shall be servant of all.
For even the Son of man came not to be ministered unto, but to minister,
and to give his life a ransom for many."

Mark 10:42–45

For I have no man likeminded, who will naturally care for your state.
For all seek their own, not the things which are Jesus Christ's.

Philippians 2:20–21

THIS BOOK IS ABOUT STAFF relationships. In particular, it is designed to help you become the effective person that your ministry needs. In an age of ego exaltation and media hype, where is the person who will faithfully serve under the leader of a ministry, seeking only to make his or her superior successful, and to see God's glory promoted? I hope that person is you who are now holding this book, and it is my desire to encourage and challenge you in your efforts.

A SERVANT'S HEART

Understanding Christ's paradox of the servant-leader is an absolute necessity for success in the ministry. The Lord Jesus Christ often used paradoxes—seemingly contradictory statements—to highlight the differences between divine and human values. He said in Matthew 20:27–28 that the one called to be "chief among you" is really called to be the "servant," and He demonstrated that leadership in the washing of the disciples' feet. By sacrificial service, Christ, the ultimate servant-leader, inspired loyalty and love in His followers. You, who are both servant and leader, are called to do the same.

Consider, by way of contrast, some government agencies that I never enjoy having to visit. Why do I dislike them so much? Because of the way people are sometimes treated at these offices. There are long lines, of course: one for this paper, one for that test, and another for payment. This is to be expected. But no one seems interested in helping. In fact, some employees seem annoyed at even having customers. "Get in this line—no, you need that paper—go over there." That lack of a servant spirit makes these offices a very unpleasant place to be. I am sure it is not like this everywhere, and

I know many fine public employees. However, in one particular office, I found no courtesy and no helpfulness whatsoever. The frustration level got so high that two men got into a fight. One cut ahead in line, the other called him names, and the other 560 of us standing in line watched the show!

Or consider a certain barbecue restaurant that I patronized on occasion. As I walked in one day, the employees shouted, "May I help you?!" The words were correct, but the timing and the tone of voice were not! They said the right words, but they did not seem to mean them. They followed what were obviously the instructions of the owner, but they missed his intention.

Then again, I once had the educational experience of attending court, on three occasions, with a new Christian in my former church. The first time there, I thought that my inexperience was the problem. I soon found out that the confusion was not all my own. I phoned ahead of time to get directions and the location of the courtroom. We arrived early. No one was there, so we waited. And waited. No one came. Then we asked. "No," we were told, "they moved this session to another building down the road."

It took as long to get an elevator at the second building as it took to walk to that building. Then no one seemed to know what was going on there, either. But we finally tracked down an answer: "No, they switched back to the other building. They should have told you that back there." We finally arrived forty-five minutes late. That was okay, however. The hearing was an hour late, so we were right on time.

Whether in government agencies or restaurants or courtrooms, the worst problem is not the lines or the changes, but the feeling that no one really wants to help. What, then, is it like for someone new coming to our ministries, or maybe even for those with whom we deal regularly?

Yes, there must be rules and procedures for a school, a business office, or an administrative office. There can be no organization without them. However, these procedures should make us better servants. People should feel that the system is working for them— not that they are caught in the cogs of a machine. It is important for us, the staff, to have a service-oriented attitude toward those with whom we come in contact, and to train and encourage others to do the same. Whether someone is calling us on the phone for counsel or is coming in to inquire about our ministry, we must be servants to those whom the Lord brings to us.

> . . . THESE PROCEDURES SHOULD MAKE US BETTER SERVANTS. PEOPLE SHOULD FEEL THAT THE SYSTEM IS WORKING FOR THEM—NOT THAT THEY ARE CAUGHT IN THE COGS OF A MACHINE.

I have often shared with those in ministry that everyone needs to have a servant's heart. We hear much about this in our Christian circles. But often in our teaching and preaching it seems we are only expecting our listeners to serve. Although this is true, we teachers must realize that we need to be the greatest illustration of serving. My goal—whether in teaching a class, or in holding a responsibility of authority on staff, or in the church—should be to serve those people that I teach, minister to, or oversee. My intent must be to meet their needs, and to make them successful. Christ said that if we are in charge, we must be the greatest servants (Mark 10:44).

This servant attitude is the greatest quality of a leader; but, sad to say, it is often the one most lacking.

I am saddened when I see people involved in ministry who act as though everyone should give them something, whether that something is a position, an honor, or a salary. Perhaps they feel that they paid the price and put in the time, and now it is their turn to reap the benefits. This is no different from the philosophy of the secular world, and has no resemblance to the kind of leadership that Christ modeled.

I met an unintended lesson in leadership at a conference many years ago. I was young and very new to the world of Christian ministry. When an older man asked me about my position and why I was at the conference, I replied that I was the youth pastor in an area church and that my pastor had asked me to attend the conference. He replied, "Son, I am a senior pastor. I don't report to anyone but God." I must admit that I was taken aback because, although I understood what he meant, I could see in him a very willful, arrogant attitude. Even as a young man with a natural tendency to respect those older in the ministry, I did not receive any positive impression from his answer.

We should appreciate the privilege of making a living while we serve the Lord full time in our ministries. I became a Christian and began serving the Lord during my days of working in management for J. C. Penney. The only difference between that time, more than forty years ago, and the present is that I have the privilege of being able to serve more, to do more, and to help more people because I have my financial needs met by the ministry. Back then, I wasn't able to be at church for some services or revival meetings because I had to work. I wasn't able to spend as much time ministering, because forty hours a week were spent making a living. Now I thank the Lord that I have the privilege of fellowshipping full-time every day with Christians while I serve them, the Lord, and the people God brings in touch with our ministry. I don't want to abuse that privilege.

A SERVANT'S PORTRAIT

Servanthood. Yes, we hear much about this term in the ministry today. This and the term *servant-leadership* are commonly used to promote conferences and ministries around the country in these early years of the twenty-first century. But what is servant-leadership? Many of us are in full-time Christian work, earning a living in organizations which have Christian ministry as their declared purpose. Beyond that, every Christian should be in full-time Christian service, even if earning a living in secular business. Scripture gives us many references to our calling as full-time servants of God (Rom. 12:1–2; 1 Cor. 6:19–20; 1 Pet. 2:5; Rom. 6:13). The idea of servant-leadership is best defined by Christ's own words and example, as seen in Mark 10:42–45.

But Jesus called them to him, and saith unto them, "Ye know that they which are accounted to rule over the Gentiles exercise lordship over them; and their great ones exercise authority upon them. But so shall it not be among you: but whosoever will be great among you, shall be your minister: And whosoever of you will be the chiefest, shall be servant of all. For even the Son of man came not to be ministered unto, but to minister, and to give his life a ransom for many."

In "whosoever will be great among you, shall be your minister," the word *minister* comes from the Greek word *diakonos*—a humble servant who sacrifices himself for the needs of others. In my office I have a plaque that indicates that I am an ordained minister, but do you have to be ordained to be a minister? Along with a diploma, Northland International University, the ministry I served for nine years, gives each graduate something a little less conventional: a towel. On the towel is the inscription, "Be Great . . . Serve." According to Mark 10:43, we are all commissioned to be ministers. In other words, in order to be great, serve God and those around you.

If those of us who now lead in Christian work will give ourselves to God and others, we will not have to *try* to lead and influence: leadership will naturally come. It has been my observation in over forty years of ministry that those of us who are in ministry are many times not truly ministering by Christ's definition in Mark 10:43; yet we are to be examples of this principle to those whom we serve.

In verse 45, the illustration goes further: "For even the Son of man came not to be ministered unto, but to minister, and to give his life a ransom for many." Isn't it just like our Lord? Not only does He command us to be servant-leaders, but He then goes on to be the example. Have the mind of Christ in following this principle. He paid the ransom of God that we might be free (Matt. 20:28). We need to sacrificially give ourselves to others so that they can be free to serve God.

A SERVANT'S COMMISSION

Paul, one of the greatest leaders in church history, had one of the best assistants in church history—Timothy. Timothy was the pastor of a local church in Ephesus, but why was he there? Because Paul had given him an assignment: "I besought thee to abide still at Ephesus . . . that thou mightest charge some that they teach no other doctrine" (1 Timothy 1:3). Timothy was a staff member following the directions of his staff leader, Paul.

In the context of this tremendous leader-assistant relationship, Paul addresses the issue we call *chain of command*. But, in true biblical fashion, he goes beyond the outward actions to the attitudes of the heart, as seen in his exhortation in 1 Timothy 6:1–6:

> Let as many servants as are under the yoke count their own masters worthy of all honour, that the name of God and his doctrine be not blasphemed. And they that have believing masters, let them not despise them, because they are brethren; but rather do them service, because they are faithful and beloved, partakers of the benefit. These things teach and exhort. If any man teach otherwise, and consent not to wholesome words, even the words of our Lord Jesus Christ, and to the doctrine which is according to godliness; He is proud, knowing nothing, but doting about questions and strifes of words, whereof cometh envy, strife, railings, evil surmisings, perverse disputings of men of corrupt minds, and destitute of the truth, supposing that gain is godliness: from such withdraw thyself. But godliness with contentment is great gain.

This passage begins with the focus on servants, calling them to honor their superiors and to earnestly serve them. Elsewhere, God's Word says to serve "heartily, as to the Lord, and not unto men; knowing that of the Lord ye shall receive the reward" (Col. 3:23–24). The chain of command in your individual ministry tells you how to operate and gives you certain special targets for your service: those above you and those below you on the organizational chart. A basic principle is given in Ephesians 5:21: "Submitting yourselves one to another in the fear of God." We must serve our Lord by serving these various people. We must do all that we can to help them to be successful in their responsibilities.

Our service needs to be earnest—just as if we were directly working for the Lord Himself. No room here for half-hearted effort—nothing short of 100 percent is good enough. Eliezer, Abraham's servant who was commissioned to find a bride for Isaac, knew that he had someone special when Rebekah not only gave him the drink he requested, but also went on to water the whole caravan of camels.

Furthermore, our service must be effective. When I think about developing the heart of a servant, I am challenged by Joseph. Think of his situation. He was unfairly put in a miserable position: sold by his brothers and bought as a slave. What happened? He made Potiphar successful. Joseph did all that he could to be the very best servant he could be, and God made him to prosper. Very early on, everyone knew that Joseph was responsible for Potiphar's success. Better than that, before it was all over, everyone knew that God was the one really responsible for the success of Joseph and everyone he served.

In 1 Timothy 6, Paul begins with the focus on the right kind of servant. Then he analyzes what causes a lack of that servant spirit: "If any man teach otherwise"—that is, otherwise than this commitment to humble service—"he is proud, knowing nothing." What a combination: pride mixed with ignorance!

We need to serve sincerely. We not only need to do what is right, but we also need to do it with a right heart. Customers walking into a restaurant and being barraged with "May I help you?!" are not impressed. Neither are people who walk into our churches if they merely hear words without seeing actions. Genuine helpfulness involves the whole person, not just the formula words.

We need to serve the Lord contentedly. Paul closed his exhortation on that note: "But godliness with contentment is great gain." We live in a society that is not very content. Worse, many people in the ministry are not content. They are looking for something better. They are striving to climb some corporate ladder within the ministry. I was happy to get out of all that when I left the business world! I still want to do the best job that I can, but my motives are different. We need to be content, realizing that God has placed each of us in our unique positions. We are to serve the Lord there by serving other people.

A SERVANT'S ROLE

In 1 Timothy 6, Paul first deals with the general subordinate-superior relationship. Then he goes on to an important, specific case: "And they that have believing masters, let them not despise them, because they are brethren; but rather do them service, because they are faithful and beloved." When our superior is a Christian, we have three important responsibilities:

- To know the leader's philosophy
- To believe in the leader's direction
- To stand for the leader's philosophy and direction

One of my favorite passages in all Scripture is Philippians 2:19–22. This passage has so impacted me that years ago I claimed them as my ministry verses: "But I trust in the Lord Jesus to send Timotheus shortly unto you, that I also may be of good comfort, when I know your state. For I have no man likeminded, who will naturally care for your state. For all seek their own, not the things which are Jesus Christ's. But ye know the proof of him, that, as a son with the father, he hath served with me in the gospel."

Do you see the beauty of what Paul is saying? In other words, he says, "I want to be with you folks, but I can't be there now. I'm going to send Timothy because I don't have anyone who is more like me than he is. When he is there, it's just as if I am there. Other people just look out for themselves, but not Timothy. He has worked side by side with me as my own son, and he really cares for you."

We are called to be likeminded with those over us. We are representing, first of all, the Lord Jesus Christ. Second, though, we are representing our ministries and the pastor, principal, or other leaders. They cannot be everywhere at once, so we represent them in capacities that we fill.

This is our privilege: to be able to serve together, and to help and encourage one another along the way.

KNOW THE LEADER'S PHILOSOPHY

When you know your leader's philosophy, you are in a position for effective collaboration. This understanding enhances your mutual effectiveness and builds lasting staff relationships.

You learn the leader's philosophy both formally and informally. Interviews, orientations, pre-service and in-service sessions for staff—all deal in part or entirely with your leader's philosophy. These are formal philosophy sessions, but there are many other ways to see what a leader really believes and what his values are.

Preaching, of course, deals both overtly and implicitly with the preacher's philosophy. Furthermore, as you work through plans and problems, as you discuss people and needs, as you evaluate projects and progress, you are continually moving back and forth between philosophy and practice.

I served with my first pastor for twelve years. In all that time, he never said, "Matt, here is my philosophy." But at the end of twelve years, I knew his philosophy. I knew where he stood on issues and where we stood as a ministry. I knew where he was going because I was under his preaching, I worked with him, and I spent time with him.

Ask yourself why you do what you do in your ministry. Are you grasping your leader's philosophy? Could you, right now, write down several statements that would embody the philosophy of your leader?

BELIEVE IN THE LEADER'S DIRECTION

Philosophy and direction are related, but they are distinct. *Philosophy* is a set of beliefs and values guiding a person's actions. Direction, as I am using the term, is the application of the philosophy, the actions resulting from it. For instance, an essential philosophical belief is that *ministry is important.* That philosophical priority may find expression in a bus ministry, a rescue mission, or in neighborhood evangelization through church families. One philosophy may have many good applications.

A philosophy should be based on God's Word. Therefore, a philosophy is right or wrong to the degree that it reflects the truths of the Bible. Not so with direction. True, directions can be right or wrong because of the philosophies they carry out; but more often, decisions of direction are matters of God's particular leading for an individual person or ministry. They are the best way to accomplish a good thing. For instance, evangelism is right, philosophically speaking. Yet certain practices used in evangelism could be unethical, and so unacceptable. But who is to say which of many acceptable means of evangelism is to be emphasized at a particular time in a particular ministry? Here, God must direct a ministry through its leaders.

Therefore, a philosophy is absolute: it is either right or wrong. But direction is variable: it is often a choice between the good and the better.

> A PHILOSOPHY IS ABSOLUTE: IT IS EITHER RIGHT OR WRONG. BUT DIRECTION IS VARIABLE: IT IS OFTEN A CHOICE BETWEEN THE GOOD AND THE BETTER.

When you question a decision or direction in the ministry made by your superior, go directly to him or her with the concern, as Jesus instructs us in Matthew 18:15. Most of the time, the problem will be resolved at that point. I have been involved in ministry for forty years now, and I have always found this method effective. When I have approached my authority with a concern, the problem normally has been eliminated. Usually I have learned that there was really no problem at all. I have found out why a decision was made, or I have clarified a misunderstanding on my part. Even in the few times that I still disagreed with the decision, the issue was not major; and the discussion reassured me of my superior's motives. If, after going to your superior, you find that there is a major difference in philosophy, or perhaps even a major difference in direction, it might be time to begin seeking the Lord's leading for a different place of ministry.

While unity in philosophy is important, variety in direction is invaluable. Solomon's wisdom, that there is safety in a multitude of counselors (Prov. 11:14), was directed to leaders, to kings-in-training. Yet, seeking counsel involves discussion, even of differences of viewpoint. When two people agree about everything, one of them is not needed. Or, as another person put it, when everyone thinks alike, nobody thinks very much. You should contribute to both the philosophy and the direction of your ministry.

STAND FOR THE LEADER'S PHILOSOPHY AND DIRECTION

You must stand for what your leader believes, because you are representing that person. Let your representation be accurate and true.

Loyalty is not a passive quality: it demands action. Loyalty speaks out for someone. Disloyalty speaks against or does not speak at all. Always speak up for your superior. I have found over the years that, no matter where one works, there is always griping and complaining. When I defend my superior, his position, and our ministry, I eliminate 90 percent of the complaining that people do in my presence. This has two good effects. First, it slows the cancerous spread of discontentment. The more attentive the audience, the more the complainer is encouraged to continue; but the more resistant his audience, the more he is given cause to reconsider. Second, speaking up for one's leader, properly done, directs the complainer to the leader—with whom he should be talking. This leads toward resolution.

Would the people around you say that you are a servant of the Lord and a servant of the people of your ministry? Would they say that you serve in your ministry just as one should serve Christ Himself? Is the cooperative relationship between you and your superiors a testimony to the praise of God? Your people expect all this of you. People who come to your ministry have chosen you over (if you want to call it this) the "competition." There is a church or a daycare center on every corner. Your people could go to any one of these. There are other Christian schools, and there are public schools for which they do not have to pay tuition.

Your people need to see that you are truly serving them, and are doing all you can to help them. The more you get to know them—their problems, their strengths, their weaknesses—the more you can help them. Yes, there will be some casualties along the way, but you need to be able to honestly say that you have tried to do all that you could to help each person be successful.

It's time to honestly evaluate your style of ministry. Are you a real minister? Are you sacrificing yourself for the needs of others? Take a look at this past week, month, or year. Are you a

> IT'S TIME TO HONESTLY EVALUATE YOUR STYLE OF MINISTRY. ARE YOU A REAL MINISTER?

genuine Mark 10:43, 44 servant: a bond slave who has no rights of his own, but only does the will of his master? You may have a position on a ministry staff, but are you still focused on wanting your own way, and set on your own self-centered agenda? Throughout my forty years of ministry, I have found that most people are easy to get along with—as long as they get their own way. But what happens when you don't get your way in the ministry or in life? If you are a true Mark 10:43 minister, the focus will not be on yourself, but on how you can best serve God and those for whom you are responsible, even when you must sacrifice to do so.

✳✳✳

Life Principle:
Be a Mark 10:43 minister.

FURTHER REFLECTIONS

Adam Godshall

Pastor, Grace Bible Church

Lee's Summit, Missouri

I BELIEVE THAT THIS BOOK on staff relationships begins at the right place – with a call to servanthood. Leadership and staff relationships are easily contaminated by pride and its desire for control. Have we over-emphasized the honor, oversight, and authority of leadership? Have we felt the weight of the biblical texts that provide the examples and admonitions of servanthood? Have we embraced the popular leadership philosophy of our culture, while neglecting the unpopular leadership theology of our Lord? Perhaps we are guilty still of "Gentile" thinking (Matt. 20:25).

It is time to do the hard work of serving. Regardless of job description, title, vocation, résumé or academic degrees, every disciple of Jesus is called to be a servant. We have received gifts and a commission to use those gifts for the glory of Christ and for the effectual working of His church. Study servanthood. Embrace it. Master it, and be mastered by it. Serving will be hard work, but by sowing the hard work of a servant, we can expect a great harvest of joy.

While this book may guide us through staff relationships, it does not promise to make those relationships easy. Serving with others will test our walk in the Spirit and challenge our commitment to Christ-like service. However, when we serve others despite flaws, conflicts, and differences, we display the power of the gospel to redeem our selfishness and to unite our hearts to serve the Lord together.

Before continuing on through this book, please take some time to study Matthew 20:20–28, John 13:1–17, and Philippians 2:1–11. Pray for the servant-mind of Christ. Meditate on the kingdom greatness achieved by humble servants. Let the Word of God convince you of the lofty privilege of lowly service.

Christ established His kingdom by serving sinners with perfect righteousness, forgiveness of sins, and eternal life. Surely our kingdom living should include the beauty of serving others. There is no hope that we will serve others, or serve well with others, unless we are overcome by the glory and the grace of Christ serving us.

Keith Wiebe, Jr.

Executive Pastor, Grace Gospel Church

Huntington, West Virginia

AN ELEMENTARY-AGE BOY I WAS talking to one day told me
that he thought he might like to be a pastor when he grew up.
"Because," he said, "I like being in charge and I'm good at talking
people into things." While insight like this either makes us smile or
groan (a groan is probably more appropriate!), it is a good reminder
that the common view of leadership and what it takes to be effective
is so different from the reality Jesus taught—that the way to true
greatness is the way of a servant. I think the reason this concept is
so easy to miss is that most people misdefine greatness. If my idea
of greatness is being served, being recognized, having my desires
fulfilled, and getting my security from the accolades of others, then
Jesus's words in Mark 10:43–44 won't really work. Jesus was not just
explaining the way to greatness, but explaining what greatness really is. The greatness we achieve by serving is not defined by many
people responding to us, but by many people responding to Him.

Christ's call to servanthood is extended to all of us, and must
be answered by a choice on our part. It is not automatic, and it is
not natural. I know that my default way of thinking and acting is to
look out for my own comfort and provide for my own needs. I do
not have to work at being self-centered. It seems that I've mastered
that skill! In fact, we all automatically seek our own interests (Phil.
2:21). This is what makes the person with a servant's attitude so
noticed and so effective. This kind of person really stands out, and is
therefore sought out. Paul, in describing Timothy's care for others,

said he did not know anyone else like him (Phil. 2:20).

In my years of working with teenagers, I can remember from time to time seeing a popular young man or lady with an outstanding personality and thinking, "Wow, they would be really great in ministry!" However, the key to effective ministry in the lives of others is not personality, but submission. There are people who are more naturally outgoing "people persons," but there are no natural-born servant-leaders. It is a calling that all Christians have, but a choice not all make.

Those who answer God's call and choose to be a servant-leader find that it is not merely changing what you do, but changing who you are. Paul described Timothy as *genuinely* caring for others (Phil. 2:20). I do not think Timothy was fake or selective with his concern for others. It became part of his DNA. I cannot consider myself to have answered God's call to servanthood if I serve only when I am "on the clock" in my pastoral role, then slip into my old self-centered habits when I am home with my family, or around those I find less-than-pleasant.

In my own quest to answer God's call to servanthood, I have adopted Onesiphorus as my role model. In 2 Tim. 1:16–17, we read that Onesiphorus worked hard to encourage and support Paul. Onesiphorus frequently refreshed Paul, even traveling to Rome and diligently searching for Paul when he was in prison. Apparently, loving and serving Paul at this time was a hard thing to do: Paul was not the most popular person to be associated with, because of his imprisonment. We get just a hint of the influence that the example of Onesiphorus had on others, when Paul asks for mercy on his household (v. 16) and gives them a special greeting at the end of his letter (2 Tim. 4:19). Paul also indicates (v. 18) that the testimony of Onesiphorus was well known at Ephesus. We all have times of spiritual imprisonment, and we need people like Onesiphorus in our lives. We need those who will seek us out to encourage us and offer us spiritual refreshment. Let us also remember that those around us, especially those in spiritual leadership over us, need us to be an Onesiphorus to them.

AM I TO UNDERSTAND,
WILLIAMS, THAT YOU NO LONGER
WISH TO SERVE AS MY
ASSOCIATE PASTOR?

CHAPTER 2

THE CALL TO A RELATIONSHIP

Endeavouring to keep the unity of the Spirit in the bond of peace.

Ephesians 4:3

But now hath God set the members every one of them in the body, as it hath pleased him.

1 Corinthians 12:18

And let us consider one another to provoke unto love and to good works.

Hebrews 10:24

ISN'T IT TRAGIC WHEN THERE is fighting within the ministry? Many ministries have people bickering about who is in charge, who is responsible for this, or who has authority over that. This kind of power struggle is understandable in the secular world, but not among Christians. When we are called to the ministry, we are called to a relationship with our fellow servants. In Ephesians 4:1–3, Paul provides a look at that relationship:

> I therefore, the prisoner of the Lord, beseech you that
> ye walk worthy of the vocation wherewith ye are called,

With all lowliness and meekness, with longsuffering, forbearing one another in love; Endeavouring to keep the
unity of the Spirit in the bond of peace.

This chapter on relationships is foundational to all that follows.
My life has had changes over the years. I have lived in a city in the
Midwest, and also in rural Wisconsin. I changed from being an associate pastor to being a college administrator. In both roles, I served
under the leadership of another. Where I once answered to a senior
pastor, I then reported to a college president. I never considered my
position to be an inferior position to that of my supervisor. I knew
that God had called me to that position. Furthermore, I knew that
I could function in those positions on the strengths of my gifts and
abilities, that I could glorify God, and that I could be an encouragement and a help to those in leadership over me. In essence, I had
maximum effectiveness with minimum weariness as I functioned
in my God-ordained role, using abilities He had given me.

In my various ministry roles, I have had contact with hundreds of ministries over the years. I am more emphatic now than
ever about the importance of relationships in successful delegation.
When a responsibility is given, sufficient authority to carry out that
responsibility must also be given. Along with responsibility and
authority, accountability from the subordinate to the superior completes the process. Delegation is essential for the leader to move a
ministry forward.

To keep the unity of the Spirit in the bond of peace, at least
two spiritually-minded people are needed. Who are these two? The
leader and you. Whether you are called *vice president, assistant pastor,
associate pastor, principal, teacher, secretary,* or whatever else, a right

relationship allows both you and your supervisor to exercise your individual gifts and abilities for the glory of God.

Let's look at these two people more specifically.

THE LEADER

The leader needs to be big enough to give authority along with the responsibilities he assigns. He cannot be afraid of someone else getting some of the credit. An effective leader must be a delegator. Here is a three-fold formula for effective delegation:

RESPONSIBILITY + AUTHORITY + ACCOUNTABILITY = SUCCESS

When a leader gives someone a *responsibility*, he must always give the *authority* needed to get the job done. But with the authority there must be *accountability*. If a pastor delegates a responsibility to someone, perhaps the running of Vacation Bible School, then he also must give that person some authority for running it. This might include selecting the curriculum, establishing the date and time for VBS, and enlisting volunteer help. But there also must be some accountability. The one given the responsibility must demonstrate that he is capably carrying through on that responsibility. He should keep the pastor up-to-date on the progress and problems, and provide a final summation of the project. If he is not coming to the pastor with these things, the pastor had better be checking with him soon.

Delegation misunderstood is disaster invited. Many people think that delegation is the giving of a job. Period. They look at their list of jobs to do and think, "OK, I'll give this to Harry and this to Sue, and I'll give this one to Mary and this one to Lou. Boy, now I can go do something else!" Not for long! When one person goes on to build his own private empire within the ministry and another quietly bungles the job, the delegator will end up spending more time unraveling the mess than if he had done it himself. The leader must maintain communication with those to whom he has delegated responsibility and authority. Accountability is the key.

Another word on accountability: the leader remains accountable. He can delegate some of his responsibilities, and he can delegate some of his authority, but he cannot delegate his accountability. When a leader delegates, he creates a new line of accountability from the subordinate to himself; but he remains accountable to God, to his authorities, and to the people he serves.

If you are in a position of leadership, do not let this scare you. As an overseer of the ministry and as a leader of the flock, you must multiply yourself through effective delegation. Everyone benefits through the process. Just do it right.

And everyone does benefit from effective delegation. First of all, the *work of God benefits*: more ministries minister more effectively to more people. It is more effective because people having various gifts—and here I am talking about spiritual gifts as well as natural

> THE LEADER CAN DELEGATE SOME OF HIS RESPONSIBILITIES, AND HE CAN DELEGATE SOME OF HIS AUTHORITY, BUT HE CANNOT DELEGATE HIS ACCOUNTABILITY.

ones—are used to do the work. The *delegator benefits* in being able to concentrate on doing well what he is called to do, by being less distracted by the minute details of every individual project.

Both of these benefits are seen in Exodus 18, where Jethro advises Moses to delegate some of the judging responsibility. Jethro's advice was, simply, to delegate or die.

Here is the story. Moses has a thriving ministry when his father-in-law comes to visit. Israel has seen God work miraculously on their behalf, and Moses has been faithfully leading the people. That night Moses and Jethro offer sacrifices to the Lord, have a praise fellowship, and go to bed. The next morning, however, it becomes clear that all is not blue sky and sunshine. Verse 13 reads: "And it came to pass on the morrow, that Moses sat to judge the people: and the people stood by Moses from the morning unto the evening."

I can see it now. First case: *Pacmud v. Slimetar.*

Pacmud: Slimetar here stole three of my sheep!

Slimetar: Well, Pacmud owes me an ox!

Pac: So what?!

Slime: So I figure one ox is worth at least three sheep!

And so on all day long. So Jethro asks a reasonable question (v. 14):

"What is this thing that thou doest to the people? Why sittest thou thyself alone, and all the people stand by thee from morning unto even?"

And Moses gives him a reasonable answer (v. 15–16):

"Because the people come unto me to inquire of God: When they have a matter, they come unto me; and I judge between one and another, and I do make them know the statutes of God, and his laws."

Good question, good answer. But in verse 17, Jethro comes back with a surprise: "The thing that thou doest is not good."

Not good! Not good that Moses is faithfully leading his people? Not good that they are learning God's laws? No, the problem was not the motive, but the method. "Thou wilt surely wear away, both thou, and this people that is with thee: for this thing is too heavy for thee; thou art not able to perform it thyself alone" (v. 18).

Notice who was going to get worn out: "both thou, and this people." Inefficient leadership is not good for anyone. Also notice that this is not a maybe: "Thou wilt surely wear away." Effective delegation benefits both the leader and the people whom the ministry is serving.

One other who benefits is certainly *the one to whom the responsibility, authority, and accountability have been entrusted.* We all know that the giver is happier than the receiver, and that the teacher learns more than the student: "It is more blessed to give than to receive" (Acts 20:35). We do people a service when we give them an opportunity to serve the Lord. However, we must give them the wherewithal—the authority—to do it.

Furthermore, you will not keep anyone in a key position very long unless he has some authority. If all he does is report to you while you make all the decisions, that will get old over time. To keep a good man, you must let him have some authority. This allows him to develop his talents and to grow with the ministry.

But what if he not only grows with the ministry but also moves on to establish a ministry of his own? Sometimes, a very important function of a local ministry is to develop leadership for other ministries. If you train someone, helping him grow to the place of capable leadership, and then he leaves, do not be frustrated. This may be a primary part of your ministry. God may want your church to be a source of supply for His work. As you invest your life in developing Christian leaders, you will be investing in ministries around the world.

THE STAFF MEMBER

It is vital for staff members and lay leadership in churches to be in the process of developing both abilities and godly character. I have seen repeatedly the importance of the qualities which Jethro lays out for his son-in-law Moses in Exodus 18:21, and which the ministry leader should seek in prospective staff or volunteers: "able men, such as fear God, men of truth, hating covetousness." Certainly, staff members must be people who have abilities—"able men", as Jethro said—but more importantly, they need to be people who "fear God," people "of truth, hating covetousness." The leader must be spiritually minded, not carnally minded: in other words, not only accepting the role of overseer, but willing to take the time to disciple others who accept the delegated responsibilities. There must be a good working relationship between the leader and the staff, so that the responsibilities are carried out, the needs of the people are met, and the abilities of those taking on responsibilities are strengthened.

All of this takes a growing relationship and mutual trust between the leader and those under the leader's authority. The leader must be big enough to delegate, but the staff member must be big enough to submit. He has to realize that he is not *the* main person in charge.

Understand the working of God here. God calls a man and develops within him a message. That man then gathers around him people with a similar vision, and together they develop a ministry. We must realize that the vision for the ministry—the direction—largely comes from the leader, the person in charge. As a result, most people will identify the ministry with that person. Although I have been at times in associate positions longer than the pastor or leader has been in his, the name most associated with the head of the ministry would be the pastor or president. God has given him a vision for what is going to be accomplished, and I am excited to be a part of it. God has called me to be a facilitator of that vision, and I want to do God's will for my life.

One of the most successful staff members of the Old Testament is Joseph. Despite great difficulties proceeding from grossly unfair treatment, Joseph kept prospering wherever God put him. For our benefit, God gives many details about the life of this successful servant and able administrator.

In Act One of his time on the world's stage, Joseph learns to surrender his rights. His envious brothers sell him as a slave to a caravan headed for Egypt. He has no choice about where he is going, but he does have a choice about his attitude when he gets there. If he had been bitter and complaining, he would have remained a low-level slave in Potiphar's house and we never would have heard of him again. However, Joseph accepts his condition, puts his whole heart into what he is doing, and God blesses him: "And his master saw that the LORD was with him, and that the LORD made all that he did to prosper in his hand. And Joseph found grace in his sight, and he served him: and he made him overseer over his house, and all that he had he put into his hand" (Gen. 39:3–4). Before long, Joseph is Potiphar's business manager.

Act Two has the same plot line. Unjustly accused, Joseph is not only demoted by his master but is also put into prison. Has Joseph given up on the sovereignty of God yet? Not at all! Again, he puts his whole heart into whatever he is given to do, and the path of excellence leads from the prison to the palace.

The first lesson is this: surrender your rights and expectations. Hear what Paul says in the New Testament: "Servants, obey in all things your masters according to the flesh"

> **THE FIRST LESSON IS THIS: SURRENDER YOUR RIGHTS AND EXPECTATIONS.**

(Col. 3:22a). We are to be in submission to each authority. We are to be servants. This is the opposite of the world's standard, which says, "Do your own thing. Don't let anyone tell you what to do." Each of us is responsible to those over and under us. One of the greatest paradoxes of Christ-like living is that the *greatest servant spirit* is required of us in those relationships where we have *authority* over others.

Sometimes leaders expect those under them to obey with right attitudes and to honor their positions, but they themselves do not have a servant's attitude toward those over them. This just does not work. We teach attitudes to those around us far more by what we are than by what we say. The message our actions send can work toward our own frustration and defeat.

The twin brother of *rights* is *expectations*. The ministry leader must beware of raising unfounded expectations by vague statements or unrealistic optimism. The staff member, for his part, should not cling to his expectations, whether they are accurate or not. He must be willing to be flexible. If he is given an assignment that he had not planned on, he should cheerfully and energetically do it. He will find that God blesses that spirit now, just as He did in Joseph's day.

Resourcefulness is the second great lesson we learn from Joseph's life. Standing before Pharaoh, Joseph declares that seven years of plenty will be followed by seven years of famine. Then comes one of those moments of dry humor in biblical history, as Joseph advises: "Now therefore let Pharaoh look out a man discreet and wise, and set him over the land of Egypt" (Gen. 41:33).

All the while that Joseph is outlining the plan that this undesignated "discreet and wise" man should enact, Pharaoh is stroking his beard and staring straight at Joseph. Even as he shared the plan, Joseph must have known that he was the most logical person to implement it. The message is this: do not bury your talents. Use what God has given you. That is not seeking glory; that is seeking service. If you have a good idea, share it; and then leave the results to God.

Joseph had a habit of diligence, and this is the third major lesson we need to get from this passage. It seems that he just did not know how to waste time. This is seen most clearly as God gives details on Joseph's management of Egypt's food crisis. In the time of plenty, Joseph traveled throughout the land of Egypt. He was continually at work, personally overseeing everything. In the time of famine, when Joseph's brothers came to buy, who was there selling? Joseph. He must have put a tremendous number of hours into the job.

Joseph poured his energies into his work because he had a testimony to maintain and a task to complete. In his first meeting with Pharaoh, he directed the spotlight to God: "It is not in me: God shall give Pharaoh an answer of peace" (Gen. 41:16). Apparently, Pharaoh got the message: "Can we find such a one as this, a man in whom the Spirit of God is?" (Gen. 41:38).

We must be wise in using our time, of course. Each of us has important responsibilities and relationships beyond our paid employment. It is wrong to neglect our personal time with God to spend time in public ministry. It is foolish to slight our own families while we minister to the families of others. If we sacrifice other important areas for the "ministry," we are, at best, misguided. At worst, we may be seeking some ecclesiastical "attaboy." This might please us now, but it will rankle our consciences in eternity. We must diligently work at each of God's priorities in our lives.

However, most of us do not have to be told to take it easy: we tell ourselves that all the time. We need to remind ourselves, push ourselves, drive ourselves forward to accomplish the tasks that God has given us to do. "And whatsoever ye do, do it heartily, as to the Lord and not unto men" (Col. 3:22–24) Why? Paul offers one reason: "Knowing that of the Lord ye shall receive the reward of the inheritance." This is a pretty good positive motivation! But knowing our natural laziness and self-will, Paul brings up a certain negative motivation just to help seal the matter: God does not play favorites. "But he that doeth wrong shall receive for the wrong which he hath done: and there is no respect of persons" (Col. 3:23–25). Being in the ministry is no excuse for doing second-rate work.

Some people use the role of assistant or associate as a stepping-stone to a number one position somewhere else. That is all right. I believe in the value of apprenticeship, and it is a good alternative to thrusting a novice into the ministry. But God also does call some people to be the support personnel in a ministry, and I have to assume that there will always be more Indians than chiefs. But do not miss this point: whether you are called to an apprenticeship or a permanent ministry of assistance, be the best staff member you can be now. Your future depends on doing God's will now.

We learn from Paul in 1 Timothy 6:1–2 that we should rejoice that we have believers as bosses:

> Let as many servants as are under the yoke count their own masters worthy of all honour, that the name of God and his doctrine be not blasphemed. And they that have believing masters, let them not despise them, because they are brethren; but rather do them service, because they are faithful and beloved, partakers of the benefit.

Being on the staff of a Christian ministry is a great blessing. We can work full-time for a ministry and have our financial needs met. The only difference between my ministry now and my ministry when I was in the business world is that I have more time to serve now. I am not restricted to after hours, working around another job. As a result I should give far more of myself to the ministry than others I know who do not have that privilege. They are good, God-honoring people, but they have to put in forty hours on the job before giving time to the ministry. They have an opportunity to show Christian love in action on the job, but also have to put up with moral garbage around them all day at work, with little or no Christian fellowship. Truly, "the lines are fallen unto [us] in pleasant places" (Ps. 16:6).

God's plans are perfect, and we will find our Christian service pleasant and profitable as we follow His plans. The wise leader will not simply make use of his staff, but will also develop them. A staff member will become much more accomplished if he knows that his role, at least for this particular time, is to carry out the vision of the ministry where God has placed him. This takes *two* big people.

***

Life Principle:

Life is relationships—cherish them. Matthew 22:36–40

FURTHER REFLECTIONS

Sammy Frye
Assistant Pastor, Yates Thagard Baptist Church
Carthage, North Carolina

OUR SENIOR PASTOR IS STEVEN Johnson. I have known him for twenty-five years and have served with him in full-time ministry for seventeen years.

Pastor Johnson is one of the finest and godliest men I have ever known. I count it a great privilege to serve with such a committed and humble servant of the Lord. I seek every opportunity I can to edify him both in public and in private. In twenty-five years I can count on one hand those who have said negative comments about him to me, and I can't remember what was said. In every case I directed the individual to Pastor Johnson, as I explained their biblical responsibility to go to him. The church body knows without question my loyalty to him and respect for him. The Scripture tells us to honor them to whom honor is due, and I have sought to do that, for I believe this honors the Lord—and Pastor Johnson is so very deserving.

As I consider my staff relationship with Pastor Johnson, a number of thoughts come to mind. First, prayer. I pray faithfully for my pastor, as I love him and recognize the burden and responsibility he carries for God's people. Secondly, praise. I praise him as my Lord leads, and I take every opportunity to edify him publicly (Eph. 4:29-30). Thirdly, patience. I realize he is a brother in the Lord and, while he is a committed servant of the Lord, he is also a man who is growing—as we all are and should be. I do not expect him to be perfect. My responsibility is to trust the Lord as He grows my pastor. I am also reminded that He has been so very patient with me over the years! Fourthly, privacy. When we have had differences, I have gone to Pastor Johnson privately and expressed my thoughts (Matt. 5:23; 18:15: Eph. 4:15). Thankfully, we have been able to work through any difficulties in this manner while maintaining a wonderful working relationship. I have apologized to him when my attitudes or actions demanded it, and he has with me (Eph. 4:32). We have a very honest and open relationship one with another. Fifthly, philosophy. Our priority is to glorify the Lord, and I believe I can best do that in my ministry relationship by serving my pastor. I do my best to support him, to do whatever he asks me to do as we serve the Lord together, and I trust that our Lord is leading him as he leads me.

I have been so very blessed to serve under a pastor who is such a Christ-honoring, God-dependent, humble, praying servant of the Lord, and a dear friend! I can truly say I thank my God upon my every remembrance of Him. To God be the glory.

CHAPTER 3

THE CALL TO COMMUNICATION

But speaking the truth in love,
[we] may grow up into him in all things, which is the head, even Christ:
From whom the whole body fitly joined together
and compacted by that which every joint supplieth,
according to the effectual working in the measure of every part,
maketh increase of the body unto the edifying of itself in love.

Ephesians 4:15–16

Let no corrupt communication proceed out of your mouth,
but that which is good to the use of edifying,
that it may minister grace unto the hearers.

Ephesians 4:29

IN THE TWENTY YEARS SINCE this book was first written, I have become even more convinced that communication is the key to building any healthy relationship. It's certainly foundational to marriage: a communication breakdown between a couple is a disaster in the making. It is vital to the family. Every parent eventually spends the same amount of time in communication with each child.

It is either in many small amounts of time throughout those early preschool and elementary years, or it is massive amounts of time spent in crisis situations through the teen years. I do believe this to be true. Communication is required for effective teamwork in ministry, too. In working relationships as staff or lay leadership in churches, communication is essential.

Every ministry has problems. In fact, where there are people, there are problems. Most of the problems result from a lack of communication. Someone misinterprets a comment and is offended; someone misunderstands a direction and a project fails; someone mistakes his responsibility and a visit does not get made. Outside opposition unifies a ministry, but internal offenses and inefficiency tear it down. Communication is the key to effective teamwork.

To develop effective communication, you must get to know:

- your leader
- your function
- your colaborers
- your people

GET TO KNOW YOUR LEADER

If you are going to be an effective staff member serving under a pastor, president, principal, or other leader, you had better know what your leader needs. We have already discussed understanding philosophy and direction. Here, I want to deal more on the level of daily functioning—just plain getting the job done.

REGULAR MEETING TIMES

Regular meeting times are a must at any level of the ministry. There is a need for regular meetings—both of the entire staff and between some individual staff members. This meeting format is shaped by the individual responsibilities and size of the staff. Perhaps this is a part of your organization now. If not, get it started. Ask, "When can we meet once a week for about thirty minutes?" or "Can there be a regular meeting time for communication?" You will do both yourself and your leader a favor. Meetings take a little time now, but they will result in saving much time and confusion later.

In most ministries, every time something comes up requiring communication, the assistant tries to get to see the leader immediately. This wastes time in three ways.

> A FRAGMENTED TASK TAKES MORE TIME THAN A BLOCKED-TIME TASK.

First, it breaks into whatever project the leader was working on. A fragmented task takes more time than a blocked-time task. Second, the leader often is not immediately available, and the assistant wastes his time waiting for the meeting or the project needing input is delayed. Third, five short, miscellaneous meetings will take twice as long as one well-organized meeting dealing with the same five points.

A good step in preparation for these meetings is to make note of problems or questions as they come up that do not have to be dealt with immediately. This can be done electronically or by simply jotting things down on a planner or a pad of paper. In doing so, I am developing an agenda for my next regular meeting with my immediate supervisor. Sometimes I will have a whole list of things to discuss.

I am giving him a capsule update of various aspects of the

ministry in which he has not personally been involved. I want him to know the status of the projects he has delegated to me. If he has a question or problem, we talk it over then. We do not wait until the day of the event—or the catastrophe! He also has a list of things he needs to bring to my attention. This is a time for very open communication. It normally takes about an hour; then we go on to our individual duties. He is very busy in his ministry, and I am very busy in mine.

If something critical comes up, I do not mind asking him immediately. Likewise, I am always available when he wants to see me about something. Neither of us minds this kind of immediate communication; but I have found over the years that with a weekly communication time, very few urgent, immediate meetings are needed.

I also find that writing down questions and giving updated reports on projects for joint staff meetings help greatly in overall communication. Everyone leaves the staff meeting feeling like they are up to date on all facets of the ministry. As a result, they are able to transfer the information to others. This is much better than the "I don't know; that's not my department" approach that we all despise when we go shopping.

DO/REPORT/ASK

How much should you do on your own? Three levels of operation, different in every relationship, make a healthy, efficient working relationship. First, there are things that you just do. You know you are supposed to do them; you know how they should be done; and you know that your superior does not care about the nitty-gritty details, as long as they get done. Second, there are things that you do and report. These are things that are clearly your responsibility and you know what is expected, but they are not routine. They are important enough that the one over you needs to know what has happened. Third, there are things which you ask about before doing. You need to get input, counsel, and direction.

The more you and your superior get to know each other, the better you understand what kind of tasks fit into which category of action. Furthermore, the longer you work with someone, the more tasks shift from the *ask* category to the *do* and *do and report* categories.

Because it is a growing relationship, though, you must start from scratch. Early in my ministry, I had worked with our church's first pastor for twelve years. I pretty well knew what he was interested in knowing and what he would rather that I just took care of on my own. I was associate pastor and school administrator and was involved in just about every function of the ministry. Then God called him to a ministry in Florida, and I handled all of the communication with the people of the church and the deacon board for two and a half years between pastors.

When the new pastor came to fill the pastorate, I had to start all over again. It took more time and more communication. He had to get to know what I would do and how I would do it. I had to get to know what he wanted and how he wanted it done. After a while, I began to see what he preferred that I do on my own, what I could do as long as I kept him abreast of the actions, and what I really needed to check with him before doing.

And guess what: they were not the same things as with the

first pastor. Even among good relationships, every relationship is different.

One additional note: be the bad guy when you can. Let me explain. In any ministry there are going to be times when someone has to do hard things. Perhaps you have a Christian school. The principal should be the one to expel a student, not the pastor, especially if the family is part of your church. The pastor, although he must be in agreement with the action, should be as far removed as possible from the implementation. This leaves him free to minister to the family. Of course, there are times when the pastor must be the prime mover in an action that may not immediately win friends. If church discipline must be brought upon a member, the pastor must take the lead. No pastor worthy of his shepherd's staff will try to pass that buck. But as much as you can, take the initiative in implementing the difficult decisions.

THE VIRTUE OF LONGEVITY

The longer an associate works with a pastor, or a teacher with a principal, the more effective the relationship should become. This is a blessing to the staff member because it allows him to grow. It is a blessing to the leader because it frees him to better do what he must do. And it is a blessing to the work of the ministry because it presents a case study of the church as a body "fitly joined together," cooperating harmoniously to accomplish the great task of serving the Lord.

GET TO KNOW YOUR FUNCTION

Years ago, when I was serving as the principal of Tri-City Christian school, we had an embarrassing incident. Our high school basketball team was ready for a Tuesday afternoon game with another school. The fans were there. The cheerleaders were there. But no opponents. The other school had a new athletic director, and no one told him that a game had been scheduled for that day. Knowing who is supposed to do what and using proper channels of communication can avoid this disaster—and worse. In this era of cell phones, texting, and automatic updating of calendars, fewer breakdowns occur. Yet I still find that knowing one's function and checking on lines of communication is imperative.

THE JOB DESCRIPTION

The key to knowing your function is the job description. Everyone in the ministry should have one. It tells, in brief form, what the staff member in that position is supposed to do. A job description can be created in

> THE KEY TO KNOWING YOUR FUNCTION IS THE JOB DESCRIPTION. EVERYONE IN THE MINISTRY SHOULD HAVE ONE.

two ways. Commonly, the supervisor will write it out and give it to the person he is hiring. For teachers in the Christian school, the teacher's handbook is normally such a job description. An alternative is for the person entering the position to write his own. After being told his duties and after functioning in those duties for a brief time, the new staff member writes down his responsibilities as he sees them. He submits that job description to his superior, asking for his review. The superior then has an opportunity to add to or to take away from the responsibilities listed.

If you do not currently have a job description, you should write one. Having responsibilities clearly listed helps avoid false assumptions by either the superior or the subordinate. If the staff member assumes that he is supposed to be doing something that is really someone else's job, or if the leader assumes that a certain job is being done although no one has been designated to do it, there is room for problems, conflicts, and hard feelings. The job description can also be a tremendous help in the event of an illness or other situation where someone needs to cover another person's responsibilities. And, yes, even volunteer leadership should have a written job description. It provides clarity to the ministry.

THE ORGANIZATIONAL CHART

Another important tool, often overlooked in Christian ministries, is the organizational chart. Secular businesses would not think of operating without one, and we should be just as organized in pursuing God's work as they are in making money. The larger the ministry, the more important an organizational chart is. It may seem very businesslike, but it helps us function and helps us keep happy staff members and volunteers because they know where they fit into the ministry and what is expected of them. All of us need to know where we fit.

The organizational chart puts down in graphic form all of the functions of the ministry in a chain-of-command order. It is easy to see who reports to whom in any situation. If someone is a teacher, he deals directly with the school administrator. If someone works in the business office, he goes to the business manager What often happens is that someone wants to go "straight to the top," bypassing everybody in the middle. This has the potential for causing problems.

It is the day before school is to begin. The new Bible teacher realizes that he needs a media projector for his Bible curriculum. The principal is not available, but the teacher just happens to see the pastor and asks him to approve the purchase. And there just happens to be a sale going on. Trying to please the new staff member, the pastor gives verbal approval for the purchase. But what if there is no money in the school budget for the purchase? The principal will have to cut out something else, perhaps something more important.

Instead, the pastor should ask whether the staff member has checked with the principal and filled out a purchase order. Even though the pastor sees the need, he should not approve the purchase. Following proper procedures and chain of command is important to making the ministry function. A pastor must realize that when he delegates the responsibility of being a department head, he delegates the authority to make certain decisions.

This is why it is imperative that, in an all-staff meeting at the beginning of each year, the lines of responsibility are reviewed for everyone. If someone goes to the wrong person, the person who he went to should refer him to the one to whom he is directly responsible. If he doesn't get satisfaction there, he is welcome to take his problem up the line; but he must go through the right channels.

The pastor has a dual function here. In most large ministries, the pastor is everybody's pastor, but he is not everybody's direct supervisor. Anyone should feel free to call upon him as pastor. But he is too busy to try to run every department by himself. Staff members should work through their immediate supervisors.

GET TO KNOW YOUR COLABORERS

The same communication that should grace the vertical relationships within a ministry is also vital to the horizontal relationships. Cooperation, support, and encouragement—facilitated by communication and motivated by love—should mark the work of the minister. We all have our strengths and weaknesses, and we need each other.

MINISTRY OF COOPERATION

Many years ago I witnessed a truly sad incident. At the beginning of the school year, a cafeteria supervisor wanted to use a freezer that was in the cafeteria. But someone from the bus ministry said, "No, that's the bus freezer. It's for the bus ministry, and you can't use it." They had a big fight over who was going to use the freezer. At that point it no longer mattered who was in the right. The wrong attitude of the conflict overshadowed anybody's rights to a few cubic feet of cold air.

The word *cooperation* literally means "operation with." The beauty of Olympic gymnastics competition is coordination: the cooperation of every muscle and nerve in accomplishing seemingly impossible tasks. We, as members of the body of Christ, should strive for the same skillful operation with every other member.

When the youth director discovers that the coach has scheduled a basketball game on the night of his hayride, harmonious relations are definitely not promoted. Such conflicts can be avoided by having a master calendar for the ministry. Once a year, all of the department heads should meet to outline the events for the next year. The master calendar is formulated. After that, all changes must be submitted to the staff. In weekly staff meetings these changes can be discussed, approved, and then the calendar updated. This avoids calendar and staff conflicts.

If you have a school, have regular faculty meetings and prayer meetings with your faculty. No one wants to be "meetinged" to death, but it is important to meet at least once a week to communicate with the different people on your staff. For instance, if I supervise the office staff, then once every other week I should meet with them to go over the calendar and anything else that might pertain to their work. In the intervening weeks they could meet without me and pray for fifteen to twenty minutes. This communication encourages staff harmony.

Write things down. Even when you have face-to-face verbal communication, that which does not get garbled in the speaking may get garbled in the hearing. Maybe you have seen this sign: "I know you think you understood what you thought I said, but what you heard wasn't what I meant to say." Good communicators accompany or follow up important verbal communication with written communication. It is always a good idea to send a follow-up e-mail summarizing what you think just transpired. On the other hand, you should never, never, never try to solve problems electronically. Problem resolution requires face-to-face meetings or at least telephone conversations. Too much can be misinterpreted with merely written communication. You can follow up by e-mail what was shared in the conversation, but face-to-face communication is the best way to reach a mutual understanding.

Purchase orders are a vital part of good communication. Have you ever had someone catch you in the hallway and want to buy bulletin board supplies for school? Right then you are on your way to chapel, due to speak in two seconds. "Bulletin board supplies," you think. "That sounds pretty small." So you say, "OK, go ahead." Unfortunately, this individual is thinking big time! Next month brings in a $200 invoice, and you ask, "Who ordered this? How are we going to pay for it?" When you track down your prodigal staff member, he says, "Don't you remember? You approved that one day in the hallway."

Yes, the procedure takes time, and usually "it" is needed by four o'clock that same afternoon; but slowing things down usually helps more than it hinders. It gives time to evaluate the availability of funds and the urgency of one need as compared to another, and it gives time to get comparative bids.

Have staff meetings; write things down; use purchase orders. Do whatever it takes to communicate clearly and consistently so that you can effectively work together as a staff.

MINISTRY OF SUPPORT

Assuming that God did not act randomly when He brought together your staff of unique individuals, you need to be selfless enough to help others and humble enough to receive help from those around you. We are not made to go it alone. The Scripture is full of statements about the interactive nature of Christian work:

> And I intreat thee also, true yokefellow, help those women which laboured with me in the gospel, with Clement also, and with other my fellow-labourers, whose names are in the book of life. (Phil. 4:3)

Take Mark, and bring him with thee: for he is profitable to me for the ministry. (2 Tim. 4:11)

For if they fall, the one will lift up his fellow: but woe to him that is alone when he falleth; for he hath not another to help him up. (Eccl. 4:10)

If you see a fellow staff member having a hard time with something, help him out—especially if that is one of your strengths. Your help will surely be appreciated. And do not be afraid or ashamed to ask for help.

Think back to your first day on any new job. Maybe you came to work excited about the new position, only to find out that there was no one there to tell you how to do it.

I worked in an electrical parts factory for three summers during my college years. On the first day I was told what to do: "Clean these parts in an acid bath and load them into a punch press." But no one told me that there were gloves for handling these metal parts that were covered with sharp burrs. No one told me that there were boots to prevent chemical burns as the acid dripped on my feet when I carried the parts to the press. I was thankful for a good-paying job and I did not want to be a complainer, so it took two days of torn-up hands and acid-burned feet for me to find out that there was a better way.

Take time for new staff members. Do more than say, "Call if you need me." Be there. Seek out needs, inquire, check up. Have them over after hours for fellowship. They will appreciate your support.

MINISTRY OF ENCOURAGEMENT

The devil is going to do all that he can to discourage staff members. If we do not care enough to encourage one another, who will?

> Heaviness in the heart of man maketh it stoop: but a good word maketh it glad. (Prov. 12:25)

> And let us consider one another to provoke unto love and to good works. Not forsaking the assembling of ourselves together . . . but exhorting [encouraging] one another. (Heb. 10:24–25)

Words are powerful, and the gift of speech is one of the unique gifts of God to the human race. Let us use our words wisely.

It is clear enough that we should give encouragement. A pat on the back, a comment on a job well done, consolation in the hard times that "even this shall pass away," prayer together—there are many tools of encouragement. But what about you: what happens when you need encouragement? One more verse: "Give, and it shall be given unto you; good measure, pressed down, and shaken together, and running over, shall men give into your bosom" (Luke 6:38).

Be an encourager.

GET TO KNOW YOUR PEOPLE

It is important to get to know the people in your ministry. True, you may not be the senior pastor; but you need to know, love, and care for them.

Some years ago our senior pastor was gone to the mission field for two weeks. During that time a family in our church had a still-born baby. This was a very difficult situation, but the pastor was not there. What do you do—wait until he comes back? No, you have to go on as one of the shepherds or leaders of the flock. You get counsel and give comfort and meet the needs. I knew the family well, and that made it easy for me to step in. I did not feel awkward, and they did not feel slighted. They needed to know that I knew them and loved them; that I was likeminded with our pastor; and that when I had the graveside service for that little baby, it was the body of believers ministering to one another.

Even if you are not a pastoral staff member, you need to get to know the people you serve. Show them love with impartiality; show them concern.

> **THE TWO MAIN REASONS PEOPLE VISIT A CHURCH ARE FOR (I) FRIENDS AND (2) A PLACE TO SERVE.**

Perhaps you will see a need that you can meet: do it. Perhaps you will see a need that ought to be referred to the pastor: write it down and give it to him. Then follow up. Even if the pastor or another staff member is involved, write a note or make a telephone call of encouragement to show your concern. The more we get to know our people, the more effective our ministry will be to them: and people need to know that we care.

Some years ago I did a study of why people visit a particular church. You would think the drawing factor would be good doctrine. It isn't. The people we need most to reach are the ones who are not spiritually mature enough to recognize the importance of sound doctrine. The two main reasons people visit a church are for

(1) friends and (2) a place to serve.

Sometimes I visit someone who visited our church recently and liked the church, but is still looking around. He might offer as a reason that he is not sure he believes just as we do or that the church is too large, but the real reason is that we needed to do a better job of caring for him. If someone had taken the time not merely to shake hands but to invite him to a particular Sunday school class, to invite him for fellowship in the home, or to introduce him to several others in the church, he probably would not have continued to look. Statistics prove that a person makes up his mind concerning a return visit in the first fifteen minutes of the first visit.

SIX MONTH CRITICAL PATH

A pair of studies done by Church Growth Inc. analyzed the needs of people in their first year at a church. These studies showed that most people who leave a church do so within the first year. Much of the cause of that departure is seen in the analysis of the needs of the newcomers in two distinct six-month periods.

1. During the first six months, people are looking for quantity relationships. They are asking questions such as, "Can I make friends?" or "Do I fit in?" This is sometimes called the six month critical path because it is vital for people to build friendships with others during those early months of visiting a church, even if they have become members.

2. During the second six months, people are looking for quality relationships. They are asking themselves questions like, "Are my new friends as good as my old friends?" or "Is my contribution valued here at the church?"

Understanding these two phases helps us meet the needs of people who are new to our ministries. Small groups can incorporate people better than large groups. We should break down our churches into smaller groups so that people can more readily move beyond surface relationships to build genuine friendships. Another way to use these findings is to simply practice building friendships—and to exhort others to do so. Are you seeking to build friendships with those who are new to your church, or are you satisfied with your present friendships, not trying to build bridges to others? Are you encouraging others to also build these meaningful and ministering friendships?

Doctrine is of supreme importance, but most people are not focusing on that. I have worked on the pastoral staff of a large ministry in a metropolitan area and in a smaller church in a more rural area. In both ministries, people needed to know that people cared about them. We often say that the goals of the church are food and friends—the spiritual food of the Word of God and developing friendships with others seeking God's will and plan for their lives.

When my wife and I first began to attend a Bible-believing church, there were about thirty-five people who came on Sunday and Wednesday nights. After church they had a great

> **YOU ARE MORE THAN A PAID EMPLOYEE: YOU ARE AN INTEGRAL PART OF YOUR MINISTRY.**

time of fellowship, because most of them were related. However, we had difficulty getting to know people, because we were not of that clan. They did not intentionally leave us out. Either they did not think to include us or they were not quite sure how to include us. The fact remains that in both large and small churches we must reach out and show concern for others.

Look around after a Sunday service. You will see people migrating into little groups to talk. Look around the next Sunday: same people, same groups. We tell our teens not to be cliquish, but I am not sure how good an example we adults are. Look more closely, then. You will see a few other people who just drift out. They are not going to stand around long with no one talking to them; they are going to get into their cars and head out. And no one really has cared for them. Oh, the message was good. The people seemed friendly and shook their hands. But if after a few weeks all they get is handshakes, they will be gone.

What does all this have to do with you, if you are a second-grade teacher or a secretary? It's all part of being an effective member of the ministry team. You are more than a paid employee: you are an integral part of your ministry. Whatever you are paid to do, serving is the bottom line.

Communication is the key to harmonious staff relations. It is the key to making your ministry a joyful place to work. While God never promised that the ministry would be easy or that it would always be fun, it is certainly His plan that it should be a joy to walk in on Monday morning, look a staff member in the eye, and say, "It's good to see you, brother."

***

Life Principle:
Edify and build others up. Ephesians 4:29

FURTHER REFLECTIONS

Morris Gleiser

Evangelist

Indianapolis, Indiana

IT WAS 1992 AND IT was the first heat of the 400-meter run. Derek Redmond was there to represent the United Kingdom at the Barcelona Summer Olympics. Derek broke from the pack and quickly seized the lead, when he heard a pop in his right leg. He fell down lame with a torn hamstring. What happened next is now one of the climactic moments in Olympic history. From the top of the Olympic stadium, Derek's father, Jim, began to make his way down to the bottom of the stands, sidestepping people and bumping into others. He had to be with his son. By this time, Derek had pushed away the medical crews and had begun to hobble on one foot around the track. He was determined to finish his race, even though he was out of the running for a medal. The crowd of 65,000 spectators rose, *en masse*, to cheer Derek's efforts. Finally, Jim Redmond made his way onto the track, pushing away the security guards and running to his son's side. He put his arm around his son, holding him tightly and said, "I'm here, son; we'll finish together."

There is something in that story that deeply moves me and reminds me of the need for people in ministry to recognize that we're on the same team, fighting the same enemy, and needing to encourage each other in our respective races.

The Lord tells us in Ephesians 4:11–13 that He has gifted men to be prophets, apostles, evangelists, and pastor-teachers . . . "for the perfecting of the saints, for the work of the ministry, for the *edifying of the body of Christ.*" When a staff member uses his or her gifts in the local church, it will bring about edification; i.e., it will bring about growth in others. The entire church family is built up and strengthened when individuals find their gifts and then use them. The communication of these gifts may be through a speaking gift; however, many times the communication comes through a serving gift.

The bottom line is this: *true leaders are servants.* We are here to serve one another. This will always go against the grain of our thinking and living. There is a natural bent to our life that says, "I want to be recognized, appreciated, awarded, noticed, and advance." That's what is natural; it is *super*-natural to serve others, and that is exactly what we should be doing in our respective ministries. We ought to be walking in the Spirit, in order to use our gifts to better serve others.

Marriages suffer when spouses don't walk in the Spirit. They mistreat each other, fail to effectively communicate with each other, and grow distant from each other. The same thing is true among God's people in the work of ministry. Staff members will become critical of one another, grow distant from one another, and bring reproach to the Lord's name and cause. Once again, we are in this family together; we are in this war together. We must seek to serve one another.

On the more practical side, let me conclude by saying that we ought to enjoy one another, recognizing what others bring to the table. When possible, we ought to express our appreciation to those with whom we serve alongside, for what they do and how they are effectively reaching others for the cause of Christ. Many times these expressions of appreciation can be made publicly, possibly in a church service. Many times these things can be stated in a staff meeting. At other times, the best approach may be a handwritten note or a face-to-face conversation. Expressing gratitude is a tremendous way to communicate.

Many years ago I was in a ministry where another staff member, who was gifted in construction and cabinetry, came to our home and made something special to help me and my family. I expressed my appreciation to him for his sacrifice of time and effort. He was taken aback and simply said to me, "Thank you for being thankful." It was obvious from his tone that he had not heard those words, "thank you," in quite some time, and it meant a lot to him to have someone appreciate him. I learned a valuable lesson that day. I'm to be looking for ways to encourage others in their gifts; the gifts that have been given to help build up the work and cause of Christ.

CHAPTER 4

THE CALL TO CONSISTENCY

Let all things be done decently and in order.

1 Corinthians 14:4

O magnify the LORD with me, and let us exalt his name together.

Psalm 34:3

Behold, how good and how pleasant it is
for brethren to dwell together in unity!

Psalm 133:1

WHAT DO YOU SAY WHEN someone asks for three days off to attend the funeral of a distant relative? For me, there was a time when the question was not so much "What should I say?" as "What did I say last time?" Of course, we would never tell anyone he could not go; but is it a paid leave of absence? Does it matter whether the request comes from a full-time or a part-time employee? I may not remember what decision I came up with two years ago, but the odds are that the person asking me knows!

There is no common problem area in the ministry more volatile than the charge of inconsistency. People are easily offended. Granted, spiritually mature people will not care if someone else seems to get preferential treatment, but we are not called to deal only with super-saints. Furthermore, allowing ourselves to become offended is something that most of us wrestle with to some degree. Even those in leadership must struggle to keep right perspectives. In many cases when staff leave one ministry for another ministry, it is because they felt that not everyone was treated fairly.

If you as a leader find that you battle this area, shouldn't you do what you can to improve the situation for others? Oswald Chambers, in his devotional book *My Utmost for His Highest*, summed it up this way:

> Do not be bothered with whether you are being justly dealt with or not. To look for justice is a sign of deflection from devotion to [Christ]. Never look for justice in this world, but never cease to give it.[1]

I know that many times the charge of inconsistency represents the incomplete understanding of the one making the charge rather than a real fault in the ministry. Such a case requires education, not a change on our part. However, no matter how hard we try, we will never be totally consistent. Our goal is to continually make progress. Written policies and standards will help us move much closer to genuine consistency in our ministries.

---

1   Oswald Chambers, *My Utmost for His Highest* (New York: Dodd, Mead, and Company, 1935), 179.

DESIRE-DECISION-DIRECTION-DESTINY

The work of God in the development of ministries seems to follow a consistent process. God puts within a person's heart a *desire*. That person makes a *decision* which sets the course of action for the ministry—its *direction*. As the ministry develops, others become involved as a leadership team and as staff members. During these times of change, there must be a consistency in maintaining the original vision and mission of that ministry. This all leads to the impact, longevity, and *destiny* of the ministry. In Exodus 18:21, we see how to grow a ministry with that consistency: "Provide out of all the people able men, such as fear God, men of truth." We must have people with abilities, and even more, we must have people with spirituality. This matched set of qualities is the foundation for maintaining a ministry. In administrative meetings over the years in ministry, the discussion has often lead to some basic questions:

- "What is our mission?"
- "What are our core values?"
- "In this matter, how can we fulfill the mission and live out the core values to which God has called us?"

As I became part of the administrative team of Northland Baptist Bible College in 2004, I was impacted by four words on a seal, which was displayed on the chapel pulpit, articulating four core values of Christian living. Without these values, no believer will be successful as a soldier in spiritual warfare. As you consider the importance of consistency in a ministry and in the individual lives of ministry leaders, you can evaluate your own life and work in terms of these four qualities. Are you using these strengths to empower God's mission for your life?

1. Honesty—Being transparent with God, and appropriately transparent with others, about my life.
2. Obedience—Doing what I should do, when I should do it, in the way it should be done, with the right heart attitude to the authority asking me to do it.
3. Wisdom—Seeking daily from God's Word the abilities, skills, and insights necessary for living a life that honors and glorifies God.
4. Service—Investing my life, talent, time, and treasure for the glory of God and the good of other people.

I believe that these four statements are crucial in setting a pattern for consistency in what we are to be as individuals, and what we are to be as leaders involved in directing ministries. Review these periodically and evaluate your progress.

THE NEED FOR POLICIES

THE PURPOSE FOR POLICIES

The goal of our policy handbook is stated in the introductory letter: *"Behold, how good and how pleasant it is for brethren to dwell together in unity!"* (Psalm 133:1). More than just a timesaver with answers to common questions, the policy handbook lets people see what is expected of them and what they should expect from the ministry. There are too many little details to be remembered from oral communication. Having the policies written down greatly blunts one of the devil's favorite prods: unfulfilled expectations. Do you have a policy handbook for your staff? If you don't, I encourage you to begin putting one together.

The policy handbook gives you a chance to do much more than simply state policies. It is a detailed introduction to the heart and inner workings of the ministry. In the policy handbook that we developed some years ago, these topics were covered:

- History of this local ministry
- Organizational chart
- General policies (church attendance, etc.)
- Definition of full-time and part-time employees
- Business policies (days off, etc.)
- Basic standards of conduct for staff

The detailed table of contents is given in the appendix to offer ideas of what to cover in a policy handbook.

PRODUCING POLICIES

In developing policies, you cannot just photocopy someone else's book and put your name on the cover. Each ministry is unique and demands its own unique balance, blend, and expression of policy. Several years ago I called around to various churches and got as much input as I could. Then, prayerfully, I put together the ideas that seemed most suitable for our ministry. This is an area worthy of your best attention, because people who work with you in your ministry are worth your best attention. We review our policies once every year in a meeting with all of our employees, and give each an updated copy of the policy handbook. Compassionate, consistent policies are very important in working with people.

THE NEED FOR STANDARDS

Policies deal with money, materials, and management. They are of practical interest only to the paid staff of the ministry. Standards deal with matters of personal testimony that affect all members of the ministry. For instance, whether we take Columbus Day as a holiday is of little interest to most of the people who worship and serve together. However, there are certain patterns of behavior that can concern everyone. Standards touch on matters that affect the testimony of an individual and of a ministry. They corroborate or contradict our message in the eyes of the staff and community.

Standards are not unique to Christian ministries. When I was in management for the J.C. Penney Corporation years ago, there were standards. Not only did the corporation have standards, but individual stores had their standards as well. The difference between the standards of the business world and the standards of your ministry is not so much the kind of things dealt with as the source and motive of the standards. The business world proceeds from the contemporary expectations of society. The Bible is the Christian's source of standards. The motive of the business world is to win contracts and build contacts. The motive of our ministry is to seek to follow Scripture in our being salt and light to society.

PURPOSES OF STANDARDS

In the days of the judges, "every man did that which was right in his own eyes" (Judges 17:6) without a whole lot of positive results. Our standards of conduct attempt to do two positive things for the ministry: we want to be right with God, and we want to be right with people.

There are two main categories of standards which need to be addressed. The first category of standards deals with areas of clear right and wrong. The goal of these standards is simply to keep the individual and the ministry right with God. As leaders, we are responsible not only for our own actions but also for what we permit to become the norms in our ministries. Achan's sin is indicative of the deadly potential of "sin in the camp" (Joshua 7). Because leadership was not carefully seeking direction from the Lord when one person sinned, God said, "Israel hath sinned...Therefore the children of Israel could not stand before their enemies...neither will I be with you any more, except ye destroy the accursed from among you." Strong words! But how much more are our ministries liable to hear God's condemnation if we permit those holding staff positions to model sinful behavior! *"My brethren, be not many masters, knowing that we shall receive the greater condemnation"* (James 3:1).

The second category of standards deals with doubtful things. In this category, the two main motives still apply: to be right with God and right with people. Biblical principles apply; but even sincere, separated people differ in exactly how to apply

> OUR STANDARDS SHOULD NOT BE A CLOAK FOR OUR PERSONAL PREFERENCES. WE ARE CALLED TO LEAD OUR PEOPLE TO CHRISTLIKENESS, NOT TO MAKE THEM CLONES OF OURSELVES.

them. Knowing there can be a wide variety of acceptable standards, I believe the goal of any ministry is to teach consecration and commitment to the Lord and His Word, but allow room for private interpretation on things that are not clearly stated in Scripture.

These matters require a balance of concern for what my personal application of the Bible principle is and the needs of the people in my ministry and the need for a godly testimony in the community. Every ministry is different, but for every rule there must be a biblical reason. If we cannot express a biblical principle and show a convincing correlation between it and the rule, we need to reconsider. Our standards should not be a cloak for our personal preferences. We are called to lead our people to Christlikeness, not to make them clones of ourselves. This is most important in our ministry to young people. We can require whatever conformity we desire, but the only standards that they will keep for a lifetime are those for which they understand the reasons. This understanding should come from the Bible. If we do not teach the biblical reasons for what we consider important standards, our young people will not make them a part of their lives. When they leave home, they will leave their standards, too, and will be left to form new ones at a time when they have little or no encouragement to do right.

THE NEED FOR CONSISTENCY

CONSISTENT APPLICATION

Policies and standards are tools for achieving consistency; but a tool is not, itself, a product. A policy or standard inconsistently applied is counterproductive: it engenders bitterness and encourages defiance. Many Christian schools exhibit this sad case. Their rule books are tremendous statements of Christian ideals, but there is little correlation between the standard and the student. We must skillfully apply these ideals and procedures to see any benefit.

The primary requirement in achieving consistency is communication. Let people know what is expected, and let them know the biblical reasons why. Furthermore, let people see that your heart's desire is to help in having a right relationship with God. The second requirement is courage. You have to be willing to stand up to opposition. The third requirement is self-discipline. You must be committed to a long-range project. You cannot state a standard one day and disregard it the next. But these three qualities are not unique to the implementation of standards. Communication, courage, and self-discipline are basic qualifications for being a leader.

DISCERNMENT IN APPLICATION

We must be consistent in a vertical direction. The consistency must apply to following biblical commands and principles, not our own application of them. Good people will disagree on ap-

> **PERHAPS MOST IMPORTANT, WE MUST BE CONSISTENT IN THE INWARD DIRECTION OF THE HEART. THIS IS INTEGRITY.**

plication of principle and it is important that we do not focus on our own standards and preferences where God is not specific. Our goal should not be to control people's lives and dictate our spiritual preferences to them. The goal of standards should be for specific practice of Bible commands, not deal with application in extra-biblical matters. This is a difficult balance and much time and counsel should be given to what should be specific requirements. We are not to dictate and take on the responsibility of individual Christians and the Christian home with our ministry. We are to teach and encourage biblical living. Many ministries have crossed the line, giving the impression that the outward appearance is most important. Our responsibility throughout ministry is to let God work in hearts through His Word. In most situations, outward application will come as a result of inward commitment.

Perhaps most important, we must be consistent in the inward direction of the heart. This is integrity. All of our beliefs and values must coordinate into a consistent, biblical philosophy. Anything else is spiritual schizophrenia. If we believe that a principle is biblical, we need to live it consistently, not just when we are around others. If our standards are hung up in the closets with our Sunday-go-to-meetin' clothes, we are doomed to powerless Christian living. If we secretly permit activities that we would be ashamed to have known publicly, we are hypocrites.

Biblical consistency is required for powerful, effective service in the life of an individual or in a ministry.

A NEED FOR BALANCE

An absolutely astounding truth about the Lord is quietly expressed in John 1:14: "And the Word was made flesh, and dwelt among us, (and we beheld his glory, the glory as of the only begotten of the Father,) full of grace and truth."

"Full of grace and truth"! Here is a fullness, a perfection of both grace—the loving, forgiving element—and truth—the holy, just element. Some of us err on the side of leniency, and some on the side of strictness; no one but God Himself has ever been full of both grace and truth. But that is the goal we seek in our policies and standards. They are not stern laws; rather, they are our best attempt to do the greatest good for the most people. We need to be both compassionate and consistent. We need to have love and discipline. Keep this in mind as you develop and revise policies and standards for your ministry.

TEST YOUR CONSISTENCY

Let's probe a little further. Let's return to those four words listed earlier in the chapter: honesty, obedience, wisdom, and service.

1. **Honesty: Are you honest with God, with yourself, and even with others about your spiritual condition?** Being a part of the local body of believers is having a place to be open and transparent with others. Have you ever noticed that everyone at church is fine? Just ask the question, "How are you today?" What is the response? Most likely, "Fine." A couple of years ago a good friend asked me that question on Sunday as I walked up the aisle at church. My immediate response was "I'm fine. How are you?" Two pews later I was rebuked by my untruthful responses. I was going through a difficult situation at the time and really needed some help. So I finally walked the two pews back and asked that brother if he would pray with me about the situation. By being transparent, I entered into the strength which God built into the local church, a group of believers bearing one another's burdens. Does this type of situation happen with your co-workers and with those involved in your ministry?

2. **Obedience: Are you attentive to God's promptings and obedient when He speaks to you?** What has he been speaking to you about recently? What have you done about it? And have you been willing to share it with others?

3. **Wisdom: Are you growing in wisdom?** A simple definition for *wisdom* is "seeking God's wishes and responding to them." Have you been biblically wise in your choices? Can you name a recent decision that would have been made differently if it weren't for your commitment to honor God?

4. **Service: Have you been involved in service this week?** Have you been investing your life, talent, time, and treasure

for the glory of God and the good of other people? What specific actions can you point to as demonstrations of that servant's lifestyle?

***

Life Principle:

Seek to be consistent all the time, for His name. Psalm 34:3

FURTHER REFLECTIONS

Mark Widmer

Administrator, Romeoville Christian School

Romeoville, Illinois

MATT WILLIAMS SPEAKS ON THIS topic from nearly 40 years of ministry experience. His combination of business, church ministry, and college ministry give him a high level of credibility. It is one of the blessings of my life to have worked beside Matt for eight years. He is a model of what he writes about. Matt has truly been my mentor, whether he realized it or not.

It is extremely important that consistency be modeled in our ministries. Recall the parable that Jesus gave regarding the laborers who worked for various portions of the day, yet all received the same pay: a full day's wage. Note how irate the workers were who had labored all day. Though they received a fair wage, they felt slighted due to the master's generosity to workers who labored for a shorter amount of time. The need for consistency is amplified in today's culture, where people are all too eager to complain (at a minimum), and even to litigate in courts all across the nation. Too often, people have an entitlement attitude: a self-centered belief that they need or deserve special treatment. A well-written and often-reviewed policy manual is a <u>necessity</u> for any organization. When people know what is expected and required of them, and also have confidence that their expectations will be fulfilled, there are far less complaints and misunderstandings from followers. It is also important that policy manuals be periodically condensed—so they don't become an encyclopedia of fifty years of rules adopted for specific situations, many of which are no longer relevant to the ministry.

That being said, there is also a need for a ministry to exhibit its compassionate heart, by making exceptions to policy in some cases. Meeting a special request by someone with a need is in line with the heart of Christ. However, such requests should be documented and clearly thought through, as many who hear of the special deal will want equal treatment. This is the essence of what Matt calls "compassionate policies."

It is extremely important that a leader be known for consistency in their mental, emotional, and spiritual life. Too often, a very gifted leader has his effectiveness marginalized by such things as a bad temper, a lack of punctuality, being too hasty in decision making, or showing favoritism. The most convicting and challenging verses in the Bible for me are James 3:17-18; not being approachable, or showing favoritism, is devastating to one's reputation.

"HOW COULD WE POSSIBLY BE HAVING SPECIAL SERVICES THE SAME TIME AS MONDAY NIGHT FOOTBALL?"

CHAPTER 5

THE CALL TO COMMITMENT

By this shall all men know that ye are my disciples, if ye have love one to another.

John 13:35

Brethren, if a man be overtaken in a fault, ye which are spiritual, restore such an one in the spirit of meekness; considering thyself, lest thou also be tempted.
Bear ye one another's burdens, and so fulfil the law of Christ.

Galatians 6:1–2

Sanctify them through thy truth: thy word is truth.

John 17:17

"BY THIS SHALL ALL MEN *know that ye are my disciples, if ye have love one to another.*" Have you ever thought about his verse—really meditated on it? As I did, I reflected back to my early days as a young, zealous Christian. My wife and I would be out witnessing to teenagers on Friday and Saturday nights or taking a group to a youth rally. As teens would get saved, we, in our immaturity, would drop by the pastor's house on our way home to let him and his wife know about the decisions of the evening. Immature? Yes! Inconsiderate? Yes! They had three young children, and I am sure that they had many important things to do. Still, they never showed the slightest hint of complaint or annoyance. They were excited about our growth and our ministry to others, and that superseded any inconvenience that we caused. They manifested love by genuinely being more interested in our growth and ministry than in their personal privacy.

This kind of love is a mark of discipleship. It expresses itself in many forms. It is seen as compassion and encouragement and help. In relationships such as those between ministry leader and staff member, mutual loyalty is another expression of this love. This compassion, encouragement, and mutual loyalty are all elements of commitment. We are to be committed to God, to one another as a staff, and to the people of our ministries.

We are committed to each other because we are committed to Christ. The call to the ministry team is a call to some very special commitments. Let's look at a few.

COMMITMENT CONTROLS OUR WORDS

RECOGNIZING GOSSIP

How powerful the tongue is! Just a word, a suggestion, an insinuation can blight a name and ruin a testimony. Shakespeare made a great point when he said, "Who steals my purse steals trash; . . . But he that filches from me my good name robs me of that which not enriches him, and makes me poor indeed."

Gossip is one of the primary ways that discord is sown among brethren. God takes it seriously, and so should we: "These six things doth the LORD hate: yea, seven are an abomination unto him: A proud look . . . and he that soweth discord among brethren" (Proverbs 6:16–19).

We must first be sure that we are not guilty of gossip or slander. *Gossip* is sharing detrimental information about someone with someone else who is not part of the solution to the problem—in other words, someone who has no business hearing it. *Slander* is verbally twisting detrimental information with the purpose of hurting another (if it were written, it

> **THERE IS A TIME AND PROCEDURE FOR DEALING WITH A PERSON'S OFFENSES; BUT OUR INTENTION MUST BE TO RESTORE, NOT TO HURT.**

would be called *libel*). Under civil law, a person is guilty of slander only if the information is false. Under the law of love, a person is guilty if his intention is wrong. There is a time and procedure for dealing with a person's offenses; but our intention must be to restore, not to hurt.

But what if you are the offended party? Matthew 18 offers direction. In verses 12–20 we see the procedure of going to an offending brother, privately at first. Then in verses 21–35 we are told to forgive. This is the "seventy times seven" passage.

Gossip is a major problem in Christian circles. We tell our young people not to gossip, and then we do it ourselves. "Don't gripe about that assignment," we say, "If it is an unreasonable assignment, go to the teacher and ask him to reconsider." Nice ideal, but do we model it? No eavesdropping device has ever been invented that could overhear more than children's ears. Later that day, those same young people overhear us saying, "I just knew Mr. Snidely would do that. He's always giving me the hardest jobs in the office. I can't stand him." We have undone our lesson. However, that is not the worst that could—and probably will—happen. When they tell the story to their friends, who tell it to others, who . . . and so on, then the story "improves" with each telling. When we gossip, we create a monster. Sooner or later that monster will find its way home.

We all agree that gossip is wrong. Therefore, it is exciting to gossip about other people's sin of gossiping. This is one of the great perversities of human nature and a principle proof of the doctrine of total depravity.

LOYALTY DEMANDS SPEAKING UP

When human cowardice would keep silent, the love of Christ constrains us to speak up for our colaborer. When human pride would revel in someone's remark that exalts self at the expense of another believer, our commitment to Christ compels us to defend our associate.

Sometimes we think we are loyal when we are silent, but that is not loyalty. Silence is not always golden; sometimes it is just plain yellow. Loyalty speaks up on behalf of others. If someone is talking negatively about someone and we keep silent, we are giving the idea that either we do not care or that the criticism is unanswerable. We may even be interpreted as being in agreement. Any of these interpretations hardens the gossiper in his position and further binds him in sin.

During two long, hard months of basic training for the Army years ago, I received a lesson in loyalty. The training was hard, and our drill instructor (D.I.) was doing his job: pushing us beyond our limits. We recruits were continually criticizing this young D.I. One recruit, Eddie Williams, was different. He never complained. In fact, he even stood up for the D.I. and his motives. He could not have liked the D.I.'s tactics any more than the rest of us, but he spoke up for him anyway. Two things happened as a result. First, I felt bad about my own criticism, even though I was not a Christian at the time. Second, we all quit complaining when we were around Eddie. This lesson has stayed with me ever since.

Loyalty always speaks up. The next time someone dumps his load of garbage in your ear, try this; "Oh, I don't think that would really be the case. Have you talked to him about it?"

Very often, the response might be: "Well, no. I haven't talked to him. It wouldn't do any good."

When dealing with school or youth group situations, another cliché often occurs. You have probably heard it: "He'd hold it against my kid if I went to him."

Remind the gossiper that this person is kind and reasonable and that retaliation is not a reasonable possibility. The Golden Rule applies here: "Whatsoever ye would that men should do to you, do ye even so to them" (Matthew 7:12). Then instruct the complainer to go to the object of his complaint and discuss the problem. Give him about a week, and then check up. If he has not carried through, go with him to get the matter resolved. This forces people to be biblical. This will also cut down on the amount of gossip you have to endure. Word gets around. Be sure, however, that *your* attitude is right. You have not discovered the ultimate putdown for gossipers. You are not rejecting this sinner. You are seeking to restore a relationship between two people that you love. This is love in action.

This display of love is essential for reaching people. There is a world of wounded, struggling Christians who are bewildered by the difference between the Christianity they have heard preached and the practice they have seen. The nonbeliever looks at Christianity but often cannot see past the hypocrisy, standards, and rules. In this wicked world there will be hypocrites, and standards and rules have their necessary place. But towering above these, like a lighthouse, should be evidences of genuine Christianity: genuine love, unity, and good deeds. Both believers and the lost need to see this love in action in the fellowship of the believers.

HANDLING YOUR OWN QUESTIONS

As important as it is to properly handle other people's complaints, it is even more important to handle our own legitimate questions. I have been on the staff of two ministries over the years. Faces have changed. Over the years there have been a lot of different staff members. I have had three primary bosses. The privilege of being on staff over all these years has its root, I am convinced, in a great principle that I learned as a young Christian: if I have a question about something involving authority, I just go to that person. This policy is very important for me as a staff member in a ministry. I do not want to live with unresolved problems or doubts about the pastor or another superior. If I have a question or do not agree with him about something, I go to him.

One of two things normally happens. Most of the time, the matter is clarified. He tells me what he did and why he did it. When I see the whole picture, it usually is very reasonable. Sometimes I was misinformed or I saw only one aspect of the issue. Ninety-five percent of the time, that is what happened. A few times I have come out of that kind of discussion still not agreeing. However, what has always happened—and I mean *always*—is that I have come away understanding his motives. I see that the goal is right, and he is working toward that goal in a way that seems best to him.

These differences have never been big enough to make me leave that ministry. However, if we leave questions unanswered, they will grow beyond sane and governable boundaries. Like embedded splinters, they first irritate, then fester, then spread their infection through the whole person. The infection of deferred confrontation is bitterness. This bitterness spreads through the whole relationship and will cripple or kill if it is not dealt with. Properly handling our own questions, and the problems others bring to us, is necessary for maintaining a healthy working relationship.

COMMITMENT REQUIRES A PLAN FOR PROBLEM SOLVING

A staff member who once loved the people and purpose of a ministry does not suddenly become disloyal. There is a process of decay. It begins with pride—the development of an independent spirit—as opposed to a servant's heart. This inward change manifests itself in the outward evidence of a focus on rights and expectations. When these rights and expectations are not fulfilled, a wounded spirit results. Having a wounded spirit is a choice. All the forces of earth and Satan's realm cannot wound your spirit as long as you "let this mind be in you, which was also in Christ Jesus" (Philippians 2:5). But once a staff member chooses to dwell on his denied rights, his spirit changes. He lacks enthusiasm for his work; he needs detailed instruction; and he lacks follow-through. Another change of the heart is an uncanny sensitivity to discontent in others. The offended staff member gravitates toward others who are offended, encourages them in their bitterness, and takes on their offenses as if they were offenses against himself. The staff member must then justify his disloyalty. He may do so by gathering and exaggerating the bad reports others have against the authority. Let me put these points into one simple chart to clarify.

STEPS TO DISLOYALTY

Inward	*Outward*
1. Independent spirit v. servant spirit	1. Focuses on rights, expectations
2. Wounded spirit	2. Lack of enthusiasm; needs detailed instruction; lack of follow-through
3. Alert to discontent	
4. Justifies independence	3. Sympathizes with others; takes up offense.
	4. Exaggerates reports of others

Years ago I saw these steps occur without realizing what I was observing. Our ministry was young, and one of the goals of the pastor and the board was to provide health insurance for the staff sometime in the future. I suppose that our pastor shared this desire with a certain new staff member during an interview before he was hired. Everything was fine for the first few months. The man was an excellent addition to our staff. He was a fine Bible teacher and a man with a real heart for others. We were thrilled to have him on the staff. After a few months, however, he began to focus on the insurance. He felt that he had been promised something that was not forthcoming. He began to dwell on what would happen to him and his family if there were a major medical problem. I was working very closely with him, and this became the topic of conversation day after day. Soon I began to wonder if I had been slighted as well. I saw this sad case go from to focus on rights to a wounded spirit and eventually saw him become bitter towards the pastor and our ministry. I finally began to avoid him because I saw that he was a hindrance to me spiritually, and I saw the devastating effects that he was having on the lives of others.

This man left our ministry; and, tragically, he is not a staff member anywhere now. In fact, he is not even attending church. Others have seen him from time to time; and when they do, he usually pulls them aside to explain what a terrible ministry we have and what we did to him. Looking back on the situation, I might have helped if I would have encouraged him to talk with the pastor about the concern. Open communication in these types of situations can avoid broken relationships, as we will see in the following section.

You need to be careful to control that independent spirit. Its gradual growth, if not corrected, leads to a wounded spirit, then to building alliances of discontent, and, eventually, to the justification of disloyalty which puts a person—except for miraculous intervention—beyond recovery for the ministry.

STEPS TO PROBLEM SOLVING

Many ministries are hurting badly because people are not big enough to handle their problems biblically. We need to understand, model, and encourage the kind of problem-solving techniques that will bind up these wounds. This is a right commitment to the Lord, to our fellow laborers, and to our people.

Offenses will come. There will be times when we are wronged; there will always be a certain amount of friction in any relationship.

The Bible never indicates that we should "hold it in." We should have a forgiving spirit. "It is [a man's] glory to pass over a transgression" (Proverbs 19:11). If a problem bothers you so much that you cannot get it off your mind, there is nothing spiritual about holding in resentment. Harboring bitterness is not "passing over" a transgression. It may look better to those around us than openly complaining looks, but bitterness hidden in our hearts makes us "whited sepulchers." It will cripple our ministries; it will destroy our health; it will show on our faces; and eventually it will ooze out in our words.

We need to deal with problems—we just need to deal with them God's way. Here are six keys to maintaining a good relationship.

I. GO TO THE PERSON WITH WHOM YOU ARE IN DISAGREEMENT.

"If thy brother shall trespass against thee, go and tell him his fault between thee and him alone" (Matthew 18:15). Who should go? You. In Matthew 18:15 the command is given to the offended brother. In Matthew 5:23–24 the command is given to the offender who remembers that his brother "hath ought against" him. God is telling both parties to take the initiative, increasing the chances that someone will do right. Whichever side of the offense you are on, you should be the one who goes. You are not responsible for the other person; you are just responsible for doing what God has told you to do. Who should go? YOU.

And you should go alone. This avoids the gossip trap, or to use the biblical term, the backbiting trap. Ostensibly gaining advice, we want to involve people who are not part of the problem. We want someone else to go, thinking he can handle it better than we can.

God's plan, though, is to keep the problem solving as individual and personal as possible. Maybe it is fun to rally the troops. Maybe there is comfort in numbers. But it is not God's best for you.

2. GO AS A LEARNER, NOT AS A CRUSADER.

The attitude with which you go makes all the difference. Go with a "spirit of meekness" (Galatians 6:1). That is, go with an open mind, realizing your own fallibility, and thinking the best of the other person. This has to be genuine. Reconciliation is a function of the spirit of man. Whatever façade we put on, whatever words we mouth, if our spirit is not right, spiritual work will not be done.

3. PRESENT YOUR CONCERN.

Plan on getting to the point. This is the time for "speaking the truth in love" (Ephesians 4:15). Be tactful, but be clear.

4. SEE THE SITUATION FROM THE OTHER PERSON'S VIEWPOINT.

This requires active listening. You may even have to pull out details and explanations. Having a learner's attitude helps in this. If you make a person feel attacked, it is much harder to achieve a true, two-way communication.

The other person may have a very different perspective on the issue than you do, and you both may be totally correct. No one has a patent on the truth. Only God can see both sides of an apple at once. Often, an authority must make a decision that is good for the many, even though it may involve sacrifice on the part of some. The leader always must take in the bigger picture.

5. SUGGEST POSSIBLE ALTERNATIVES.

You have to do your homework before you go. If a problem is worth dealing with, it is worth your time to find solutions. Along with the value of your differing viewpoint, offer the value of your differing solution. Sometimes all that an authority needs is a better suggestion. If you have no plan to offer, his original bad plan may be better than no plan at all.

You also have to be flexible, creative, and diligent. Assuming that you actually learned something in the listening phase, you may have to alter your suggestions. This is flexibility. You may have to incorporate new aspects to your suggestions to meet needs that you had not planned on. This is creativity. Very likely, you will have to spend some time with the person in authority, working through the development and implementation of a better way. This is diligence. Remember, you are not launching a bombing raid. You are getting down in the trench with a fellow soldier and helping him win the victory.

6. ACCEPT THE DECISION AS FROM THE LORD.

The king's heart is still in the hands of the Lord (Proverbs 21:1). As sure as we might be, we are not always right in our ideas of what is best. Sometimes God may even have a plan for allowing someone to go in a direction that seems unreasonable. Human reasoning does not match up with divine reasoning: "For my thoughts are not your thoughts, neither are your ways my ways, saith the LORD. For as the heavens are higher than the earth, so are my ways higher than your ways, and my thoughts than your thoughts" (Isaiah 55:8–9).

Perhaps I have worked with some extraordinary people, but

in my experience I have found no cause for frustration with my superiors. Even when disagreement remained, I have come away from such meetings confident of my authority's good intention and confident of God's ability to accomplish His will.

This commitment to maintaining right relationships can even pull down some existing barriers. Some years ago I noticed that a wall had grown up between myself and a couple that I dearly loved. I had made a decision which, although it was necessary, hurt them. At first, I did not know that they were hurt by that decision; but I knew that the relationship between us was not as close as before. I could guess pretty well what the problem was, but I did not want to deal with it. However, the problem was not going to evaporate. There was no open antagonism; but there was no open love, either. This situation went on, and the Lord kept dealing with me until I could not stand it anymore. Finally, one night I went to them with a right attitude and discussed the decision. When I left their house, I was a new person. They still did not agree with my decision, but they accepted that

> LOVE IS STRONGER THAN A STRONG CITY, AND IT CUTS THROUGH THE IRON BARS OF CONTENTION, LIBERATING THE RELATIONSHIP FROM BITTERNESS.

I did not mean to hurt them. That matter is no longer a problem between us. I believe that I now have a greater ministry to that family than I had before the problem arose because they have seen me care enough to come and seek them out. I did not want to go to them at first, but that effort made the difference.

Whether you are in the right or in the wrong, it is never pleasant to approach someone who is in disagreement with you. We are warned of this in Proverbs 18:19: "A brother offended is harder to be won than a strong city: and their contentions are like the bars of a castle." Love, however, is stronger than the strong city and cuts through the iron bars of contention, liberating the relationship from bitterness.

Do yourself a favor: handle offenses God's way.

COMMITMENT PRODUCES PROBLEM SOLVERS

There is nothing wrong with finding problems, but you should not stop there. Do not just be a problem finder: be a problem solver. You need to identify the problems in your ministry for the purpose of making needed improvements. If God has laid a particular area on your heart, it may be that He is calling you to address that need. Be solution oriented, not problem oriented.

I remember one staff member who was always bringing up problems. Every week in staff meeting he would have his list of laments: "Boy, you should see the teenagers. We've got real problems in the Sunday school. Boy, we're just not reaching people like we ought to." Constant complaining wears people down. This kind of person sees all the problems, but has no solutions to offer. Why is he on staff, anyway? We are to look for problems, but we are also to look for solutions. That is our function.

A staff member who completes the assigned task is a good staff member. A better staff member is the one who exercises initiative, who goes beyond the minimum requirement of his job to see and meet needs. One who is truly committed will become a problem solver.

Joseph had already earned Pharaoh's respect as a man who could get the job done. When Joseph's family came to join him in Egypt, Pharaoh said, "If thou knowest any men of activity among them, then make them rulers over my cattle" (Genesis 47:6). Pharaoh was really excited about these Hebrews: Joseph had already made a killing for him in grain crops; now he saw his chance to do it again in livestock. He wanted "men of activity"—doers! This is the kind of person God is looking for, too.

In the New Testament we see a three-part analysis of what makes an effective staff member.

He that is faithful in that which is least is faithful also in much: and he that is unjust in the least is unjust also in much. If therefore ye have not been faithful in the unrighteous mammon, who will commit to your trust the true riches? And if ye have not been faithful in that which is another man's, who shall give you that which is your own? (Luke 16:10–12)

> THE SUBORDINATE CAN HAVE A VITAL, IN-DEPTH MINISTRY TO PEOPLE, BY PUTTING HIS WHOLE HEART INTO THE WORK GOD GIVES HIM TO DO.

1. Faithfulness in the little gives an opportunity to do more.
2. Faithfulness in money gives an opportunity to do things that really count.
3. Faithfulness in a subordinate role gives an opportunity to develop a ministry of one's own.

Here, I add that the ministry which is "your own" might not be in another place. The subordinate can have a vital, in-depth ministry to people where he is. Or he can be a nothing. It all depends on putting his whole heart into the work God gives him to do.

When I first began working as a church staff member, all I wanted was to be a youth director. God had called me to that, and I enjoyed very much working with teenagers. As I was doing this, problems would come up, things that nobody was handling. So I would go to the pastor and say, "Here's a need. Why don't we do such and such about it." He would usually say, "That's good. You do it." Pretty soon, without really trying to, I had worked my way into being the associate pastor of our growing church.

One day I was meeting with our pastor, and he told me that we were going to begin a ministry to the inner city of Kansas City. Week after week we had been bussing children to our church but then taking them back to their homes and leaving them there without any spiritual encouragement until the following week. My pastor's vision was to have a church in their community—not only to reach them, but also to teach them on a regular basis. It sounded like a great idea—until he told me that I was going to be in charge of it. I had no idea what to do or how to begin. We rented a building; and soon I was knocking on doors, inviting people to a new ministry in their neighborhood. I found that the more I became involved with these people, the more the Lord gave me a heart for this work. For the next three and a half years, I really involved myself with them and saw wonderful things take place. The potential became so great that we finally invited a full-time pastor to come in to meet the needs of the people. Faithfulness in my role as a subordinate gave me a ministry that was my own for that period of time. Today I still meet people who are products of that inner-city ministry, and I am thrilled to say that I was a part of it.

Over the many years that I served in ministry, we started several branch churches. Some of the branch churches I helped pastor; others I just helped set up. somewhere along the line I was involved in every phase of the ministry. Through it all, I have had only one desire: I just wanted to do to the best of my ability what God gave me to do. Most of the jobs that I am involved in, I have gotten one of two ways: either the pastor asked me to do it, or there was a problem and I tried to come up with a solution.

I see the associate pastor, the assistant pastor, or the staff member as someone who identifies problems and seeks solutions. His job is to solve the problems. He needs to analyze them, propose programs, and—if possible—delegate the management of those programs to someone else while maintaining oversight himself. If there is no one else, he is the one who manages the programs, too.

> **BE A PROBLEM SOLVER, NOT JUST A PROBLEM FINDER.**

Be a problem solver, not just a problem finder. In all things, maintain a high level of commitment to your colaborers and to doing the work that God has called you to do. If we simply remember the "new commandment" of Christ's, "that [we] love one another" (John 13:34), we will have no trouble controlling our tongue, reacting rightly to offenses, or seeing and meeting people's needs.

COMMITMENT GIVES US PURPOSE

I see one overriding commitment for our lives—commitment to purpose. Without this, the other commitments have no foundation. What is the believer's one overriding purpose in life? I believe that

John 17 summarizes this purpose in a prayer uttered by Jesus to His Heavenly Father.

John 17:6—The believer's position: We are redeemed out of this world.

John 17:11—The believer's presence: We are to live differently in this world

John 17:14–16—The believer's protection: We are to have no harmony with this world.

In fact, the key to all three of these truths is given in verse 17: "Sanctify them through thy truth: thy word is truth." The Word of God empowers our commitment to the Lord and to His Way. That empowerment is expressed in Psalm 119:9–11: "Wherewithal shall a young man cleanse his way? by taking heed thereto according to thy word. With my whole heart have I sought thee: O let me not wander from thy commandments. Thy word have I hid in mine heart, that I might not sin against thee." And again in Psalm 119:16: "I will delight myself in thy statutes: I will not forget thy word." God's purpose for us as believers is addressed in John 17:18–26. In summary, it says that Christ has sent us to the world.

This is our mission, our purpose. According to Ephesians 5:1, we are to be glory bearers. Whatever we do should bring glory and honor to God (2 Corinthians 10:31). In fact, Jesus states this clearly in Matthew 5:16: "Let your light so shine before men, that they may see your good works, and glorify your Father which is in heaven." This is our overriding purpose and mission.

We are salt and light, according to Matthew 5. Let's think about salt.

1. Salt is, first of all, a flavor enhancer. It seasons. We are to lend flavor to life. The believer has everything the world is craving. We must display to the world the peace of life which results from our relationship to God.

2. Salt is a preservative. Our power to preserve this world lies in our calling to be different from it. We are to act as an antiseptic rendering the germs of moral decay ineffective.

3. Salt cleanses. Salt is a pure substance. The believer is to be an example of moral and ethical purity.

4. Salt creates thirst. Our lives will create thirst for what God has done in and through our lives.

Light is the other major symbol Christ used in Matthew 5 to represent the Christian. Light is a positive guiding influence. It both

> OUR COMMITMENT TO GOD'S WAYS IS TO BE A LIVING ILLUSTRATION OF GOD'S GOODNESS AND GRACE WORKING IN OUR LIVES.

dispels darkness and illuminates. We are to "Let [our] light so shine before men, that they may see [our] good works, and glorify [our] Father which is in heaven."

Our commitment to God's ways is to be a living illustration of God's goodness and grace working in our lives. As we remain committed to God's purpose for our lives, we won't have to try to influence others, the influence will come as a natural result of living life as God designed.

***

Life Principle:

Be different on purpose. Matthew 5:16

FURTHER REFLECTIONS

Keven Brownfield
Brownfield Revival Ministries
Pembine, Wisconsin

I HAVE BEEN IN MANY conversations in which either I or someone else makes this statement: "There is very little commitment these days." As I have evaluated the statement I have come to disagree with it. I really don't believe that the amount of commitment is in question, but the object of commitment is in question. Every single human is committed to many things. So I believe it is far more accurate to say that there has been a very noticeable paradigm shift in the objects of our commitment than the amount of commitment. Let's take marriage as a case in point for this discussion. Marriage is based on a covenant commitment before God to our spouse. So if a marriage ends in divorce, that does not mean there is no commitment; it is that the object of commitment has changed from being toward God and the other person to self and some other definition of how happiness is perceived to be achieved. So, in the end, there is not less commitment—just redirected commitment.

Commitment has many levels, and if you look at lives long enough you will find that there are what I call *core* or *ultimate* commitments that should, by definition, drive all other commitments on every level. Just as the sun controls the orbits of the planets and their moons in our solar system, so *core* or *ultimate* commitments are to control lesser levels of our lives in all expressions. Part of our root struggle is that we often have a disconnect between our expression and our practice. I have electricity that comes into a breaker box in my basement. There are times that one of the breakers trips and even though there is still power in the box, it does not make it to the outlets for practical use. If we are not careful we become great at articulating our core values but very negligent at our practice of everyday life. Kind of like a tripped breaker.

While we could talk of many biblical texts that these ideas stem from, space makes room for only two. Paul, in the book of Philippians, says "for me to live is Christ." That is his core commitment that will control everything. Because of that, he goes on to inform his readers that death brings great reward from Christ. His core commitment controlled his everyday choices. In his letter to the Corinthians, he records it this way: "Whether you eat or drink or whatever you do, do all to the glory of God." Again, the core commitment controls the choices. I really don't believe we need more commitment in this day and age. I believe we need to evaluate whether our rhetoric is reality and if what we declare as our core commitments is what really controls every dimension of our lives.

FIVE KEYS FOR EFFECTIVENESS

CHAPTER 6

THE CALL TO PLANNING

For which of you, intending to build a tower, sitteth not down first,

and counteth the cost, whether he have sufficient to finish it?

Luke 14:28

Through wisdom is an house builded; and by understanding it is

established:

And by knowledge shall the chambers be filled with all precious and pleas-

ant riches.

Proverbs 24:3–4

IF WE IGNORE LIFE'S SUBTLE suggestions, life will get our attention more rudely. That happened to me once. I knew that my car battery was not as good as new anymore. In fact, after jump-starting the car twice, I even tried charging the battery for a day. But it was not until I received the phone call at church informing me that my wife and family were stranded with a dead battery that it demanded a place in my immediate plans. In other words, things do not "just happen." We must plan to get them done.

Planning is vital for getting things done, whether those things are automotive maintenance or the work of the ministry. I learned this valuable lesson years ago when I was still new to the ministry. One Sunday evening the pastor announced that he and I were going to take some prospective students to a Christian college the next evening. This was the first I had heard about my going on this trip! I was excited about going, but the first thing that entered my mind was all the work I had to do that week. I had Bible studies to teach, a teen soul-winning group I took out each week, responsibilities in the bus ministry, as well as several things that needed to be done in the office. I probably could not go. Still, after the service I wrote out what needed to be done and began to figure ways to get it done. I called people to substitute for me on projects that could be delegated. I identified which tasks I had to do myself in the next twenty-two hours and arranged my schedule so that I could do them. It was a long day, and I was tired; but when we left at five o'clock the next evening, everything had been taken care of. By planning, I had taken care of a week's work in one day.

Planning is not merely wishing. It could not be more different. Everybody longs for some goal or good, however vague; but "if wishes were horses," the old saying goes, "then beggars would ride." Planning definitely involves the longed-for end product, the goal, but planning goes further by focusing one's attention and energies on how to attain the goal. Planning involves identifying the overall purpose of a project, the activities that must be performed, their sequence, and the resources required to accomplish them.

> **PLANNING IS NOT MERELY WISHING.**

YOU MUST IDENTIFY THE PURPOSE

First, you must clearly understand what you are trying to accomplish. Why is this important to your ministry? At its highest level, this question is, "What is God trying to accomplish through my life?" We can get involved in so many activities that we never have time to discern what really counts. We exhaust our energies and expend our time and never come to grips with the question of purpose.

Without a clearly identified purpose, we are not likely to get the right job done. If we do, it will only be by the greatest coincidence or by God mercifully overriding our foolishness. Without clear purposes, we can spend our best resources accomplishing second-best goals. Without clear purposes, we can be distracted to chase any rabbit trail that crosses our paths. It only makes sense that we determine where we want to go before we get very far down the road.

When your purpose is clearly identified, you can motivate people to unite behind a cause. Jesus began His ministry by telling His future disciples, "Follow me." Why? "I will make you fishers of men" (Matthew 4:19). Nehemiah called the people to follow him. Why? "Ye see the distress that we are in, how Jerusalem lieth waste, and the gates thereof are burned with fire: come, and let us build up the wall of Jerusalem, that we be no more a reproach" (Nehemiah 2:17). Leaders must have clearly defined goals to rally people.

Purpose will rally the leader's own energies, too. I get excited when I plan some worthwhile projects that I think really can work. Some years ago when I was an associate pastor, the pastoral staff at our church designated a year as the Year of Outreach at our ministry. At an upcoming staff meeting we were all supposed to come in with ideas. I began to brainstorm. What could we accomplish in a year of outreach? I thought we ought to have a Vacation Bible School. We had not had one in years. Of course, you know what happens to the person who comes up with an idea like that: he is in charge. That was all right; I was really

> **STARTING WITH THE PURPOSE CLARIFIES THE PLANNING.**

excited about it, and we had a great Vacation Bible School. We had a preschool at this ministry. We could reach out to our preschool families with a discipline series for parents. That was a huge success. I thought of the bus ministry. We could show an evangelistic film, and reach out to the families. As a result, one of the fathers was saved, baptized, and began attending the church. We had another night for a Children's Church program in the Sunday evening service. Many of the parents came from the bus families, and three were saved that night and continued faithfully. These things were hard work, but we got excited about them. Starting with a purpose helps to clarify the planning of a ministry.

Every project, every activity, everything that you do should start with a purpose. You should be asking the question, "Why am I doing this?"

YOU MUST VISUALIZE THE COMPLETED PROJECT

Once you are set on the purpose you are trying to accomplish, you need to visualize the completion of the project. This visualization helps you see the details that need attention. It is an essential link between the purpose and the project. When people speak of a leader as a person with vision, this is what they are referring to. Great leaders can see all the details required to reach the goal. When you see the details, you can move on to the next step: planning the detailed steps to accomplish the purpose.

David visualized the completed plan as he dealt with the giant, Goliath:

> *This day will the LORD deliver thee into mine hand; and I will smite thee, and take off thine head from thee; and I will give the carcases of the host of the Philistines this day unto the fowls of the air, and to the wild beasts of the earth; that all the earth may know that there is a God in Israel.* (1 Samuel 17:46)

David could see the Lord that day not only slaying the giant, but also giving a total victory over the whole Philistine army and creating a testimony to His greatness.

In contrast, consider the salesman who was asked by his supervisor how much he was going to sell the next year. The salesman replied, "I don't know, but it will be more than last year."

"Well, then, how much did you sell last year?"

"I'm not sure, but it will be more next year."

Here is a person who does not know where he is going. He cannot see a completed goal because he has not evaluated where he is and where he needs to go. As leaders, we have to clearly identify the purpose and then visualize the completed project.

YOU MUST SET GOALS

General Dwight D. Eisenhower accomplished one of the greatest military achievements of all time. On June 6, 1944, he directed the landing of Allied troops on the German-occupied French coast. This massive coordination of manpower, courage, and cooperation turned the tide of World War II and made Eisenhower's name immortal. There were thousands of men from all of the Allied countries involved, hundreds of ships and airplanes, and four target beaches. But it all had to be planned one step at a time. Let's take a lesson from General Eisenhower: breaking a big task into little steps can make the difference between success and failure.

Analyze the project at hand and break it down into smaller, specific objectives. This is goal setting. Real, rubber-meets-the-road practicality begins here. You cannot say that you will win a certain individual to Christ on a specific date; but you can select five tracts, pick an evening, visit some people, and

> THERE IS NO NEED TO PLAN MEDIOCRITY. MEDIOCRITY WILL OCCUR WITHOUT THAT MUCH BOTHER.

present the plan of salvation. Running a bus ministry is a big job; but isn't it really just a matter of making one phone call at a time, talking to one prospective driver at a time, and so on? The longest journey not only begins with the first step, but also it continues one little step at a time.

GOALS MUST BE YOUR OWN

Adopt the project goals as your own. You must have a personal involvement with them in order to rally all of your energies to the task. The project may initially be given to you by someone else, but you must adopt it as your own. You must envision what can be accomplished in a given project and in your ministry. You must latch onto these goals as vitally important to your own life and ministry.

GOALS MUST BE BIG, YET REALISTIC

Your goals should be big enough to push you toward something you would not have accomplished otherwise. However, these goals should not be completely unrealistic; they must be attainable. Stretch yourself a little. On the other hand, there is no need to plan mediocrity. Mediocrity will occur without that much bother.

GOALS MUST BE WRITTEN DOWN

It is one thing to visualize your goals; it is quite another to get them down on paper. The writing makes you be realistic and helps you be detailed. It also helps you remember your plan and keep working on it.

Certain tools will help you write down goals and keep them in front of you. The Personal Planning Sheet included in the appendix is useful for outlining the big goals for the year. The Weekly Planner brings these goals down to the "this-week" level of planning and gives you space to list specific things to do toward those plans. Finally, the Things to Do TODAY sheet is where you list your immediate tasks. These do not take as much time as it may seem. A few hours periodically dedicated to dealing with the major goals of your life is not much time to invest—but it is more time than most people do invest. Thirty minutes to an hour a week for the weekly planner and a few minutes per day to list the things to be done today—you can afford that. In fact, I do not think you can afford to work without this kind of planning. Planning saves more time than it takes. It has been proved time and again that a little planning at the beginning of the day saves at least two hours during the day.

YOU MUST OUTLINE ACTIVITIES

It is important not only to set specific goals but also to be working toward accomplishing them. The last key in planning is to identify the activities needed to accomplish the objective. List individual jobs to be done, people to do them, and money and materials required. Then arrange these as projects in the most efficient order and give them due dates.

These plans must be specific, not vague generalities. It is not enough to say that you will have a better Sunday school class. You must identify specific needs and develop specific steps to meet those needs.

To do this, goals must be subdivided into attainable steps. The project that you desire to accomplish is the long-range goal. It may be a very lofty goal. Considering the God we serve, anything that proceeds from Him probably will be. Establishing the little steps toward that goal brings it clearly within the realm of possibility. Break the long-range goals down into short-range goals that you can actually work toward on a daily and weekly basis.

YOU MUST WORK TOWARD GOALS

Years ago when I first entered the ministry, God called me to work with teenagers. My first objective was to convert our previous church building into a teen center, The Barn. I quit my job in management and for the next month or so tried to do what I could on the building. We had no money for the project, and I did not have much in the way of remodeling skills. I really had very little to do, and it became frustrating. One day I attended a conference and was challenged to set specific goals and to write them down. I quickly left the conference, even before it was finished, and spent about an hour writing down what my objectives were and how I was going to achieve them. I broke the project down into short-range goals: fundraising, workdays to get people to help me, a target date for opening the center, and so on. When the target date arrived, we had the teen center open. Four teenagers were saved on the opening day. By God's grace, planning played a part in establishing a big goal and breaking it down into realistic, smaller, short-range goals.

A planning process is not complete until the needed resources have been determined. In Luke 14 the Lord discussed planning in terms of counting the cost. He said that someone planning to build a tower needs to first sit down and determine

> **PLANNING, LIKE ANY OTHER ACT OF DISCIPLESHIP, SHOULD RECEIVE OUR TOTAL INVOLVEMENT.**

"whether he have sufficient to finish it? Lest . . . all that behold it begin to mock him, Saying, This man began to build, and was not able to finish" (vv. 28–30). Resource planning is a very important part of the planning process.

The context of these verses points out something fundamental and important about the planning process: it must represent our total commitment. The point of Luke 14:25–35 is that the Lord cannot use half-hearted hangers-on (they cannot be called disciples if they are half-hearted). The Lord's reference to the planning process is only incidental to this main point. He is saying, in effect, count the cost—the Lord wants to use you, but He needs you to commit yourself totally to Him. Planning, like any other act of discipleship, should receive our total involvement.

This stage of planning must be extremely detailed. We must plan far enough in advance to avoid surprises. Give yourself time to check and double check everything. Do not assume anything. Remember Murphy's Law: If anything can go wrong, it will go wrong at the worst possible moment.

There must be time spent planning for the year, planning for the month, planning for the week, and planning each day. I do know that we can go to extremes, and some people spend much time dreaming and little time working toward the dream. Still, there must be a plan in order to move forward in ministry. One successful businessman said that he spends one half day every two weeks in planning. He also takes one full day per month and a couple days each year for planning. This is difficult to fit into a schedule, but it is necessary for success. "See then that ye walk circumspectly, not as fools, but as wise, redeeming the time, because the days are evil" (Ephesians 5:15–16).

TAKE A LOOK AT THE FOUR LEVELS OF PLANNING.

1. *Plan long-range goals.* This works well at the beginning of the year, but it can be done at any time. If you have not yet articulated the long-term goals of your life, the best time for you is now. Then decide on real steps which you can take this year toward those goals. Evaluate the prior year and identify what needs to be accomplished in the coming year. This keeps the big-picture goal—the mission—before you.

2. *Plan the month. What is* coming up? Begin working now on things that will be happening sometime during this month. If at all possible, begin working toward final plans for upcoming months.

3. *Plan the week.* What must be done this week to accomplish your stated goals? Have a plan set at the beginning of the week and then begin working each day from that plan. Then, starting the next week, evaluate what was accomplished and identify what should be carried into the new week's plan. Saturday is my day to plan my upcoming week. I spend some time looking back over the past week and identifying what needs to be carried forward for completion. I then look forward to the new week and what is coming up. I begin to write out my list for the week and break projects down into different days.

4. *Plan the day.* In essence, plan your work and then work your plan. Be flexible: God may have planned things that are not on your list! However, let the list be a guard against wasting your day chasing rabbit trails. At the end of the day, consider what was accomplished and carry the unfinished items to the next day.

Are you ready to do some planning? There have been days which I had planned well and then got much done. There have been other days in which I worked just as hard and didn't follow a plan, with the result that my entire to-do list was left for the remainder of the week. Other days were planned, but interruptions beyond my control caused me to get sidetracked. Planning is not foolproof, but much more will be accomplished with a plan.

SIX TYPES OF GOALS

Even people who are good at planning and executing projects sometimes get bogged down in details and fail to see the bigger picture. If we lose sight of the coordinated whole that all of our individual projects are supposed to be part of, we are in danger of becoming imbalanced in our lives and ministries. There are six types of goals in a person's life. All of them must receive attention.

First of all, there are *spiritual goals.* In your personal relationship to God, this might involve consistently reading your Bible, reading through the Bible in a year, or memorizing one or two verses each week. In relation to family, this might involve pouring energy into encouraging a spouse spiritually and handling problems biblically. In relation to work, it might involve focusing on a specific area of need in the ministry. For teachers, it may mean more consistent biblical integration into their teaching. For an administrator, it may involve providing some special chapels to meet specific needs in the student body. In relation to outreach ministry, it might involve weekly goals for witnessing to the lost or for discipling a new Christian.

Family goals should not be neglected while you meet the needs of others. You may need to spend specific time each week with each family member. Maybe you need to establish a family night just for having fun together. Maybe the need is to establish a regular pattern of family devotions.

Mental goals may include broadening your information on important issues. Maybe you should take a class, or read a book a month, or read magazine articles on a specific topic. Christian biographies are extremely valuable. Mental goals may include listening to Christian radio or recordings throughout the week or using your time more wisely than watching television. There are many things you can do to sharpen your mental skills and resources, thus making yourself more effective in the ministry.

Physical goals are as varied as they are important. They may include going to bed early enough to get proper rest or getting up early enough to brush your teeth. Maybe you should lose twenty pounds over the next six months or get into a regular routine of exercise, walking, or jogging. Perhaps there are some health problems you

> ONE STRANGE DANGER OF THE MINISTRY IS NOT GETTING ENOUGH FELLOWSHIP. YOU NEED CHRISTIAN FELLOWSHIP, AND OTHERS NEED YOU.

keep putting off because they are not urgent—and, if you are totally honest, because you are afraid to deal with them.

We all should have *financial goals*. You need to look at your finances, figure out where you are, and decide where you need to be. This might mean setting aside money for a new car now, before the old Model T cranks its last. It might mean saving for a family vacation, an appliance, or the children's college education. Figure how much money you can put aside each week, and then stick to it.

You need to set *social goals*, too. This is fellowship. One strange danger of the ministry is that you can get so involved in working with Christians that you do not have time for fellowship. You need Christian fellowship, and others need you. Set aside time to have people into your home at least once a month. Get involved in church activities or programs that will help you get to know others. Fellowship is a vital part of the Christian life, and it is a key source of encouragement.

In conclusion, goals are a must. However, they are nothing new. You accomplish goals every day as you get up, get dressed, and get to work. You do not think of these as goals because they are habits.

You need to consciously develop other habits that will make your life more effective and fulfilling. Make the attaining of goals a daily part of that habit. Make goal setting work for you.

***

Life Principle:

Plan your work; then work your plan. Ephesians 5:15–16

FURTHER REFLECTIONS

Wynne Kimbrough
Pastor, Grace Baptist Church
Kingsford, Michigan

WE ALL HAVE A TENDENCY to go to extremes. When it comes to planning, this is no less true. And it is especially true in the ministry. We can tend to live in unbalanced extremes. This can be seen on the one hand when we let our days be a continual open-ended "trust" that whatever happens is the will of God for that day—with no planning, no forethought, no vision, and in most cases, only the sheer grace and mercy of God that real ministry ever takes place. The other extreme is *my plans*, where I have every moment of the day meticulously outlined for greatest efficiency, and interruptions are not tolerated. This is obviously a hindrance to true ministry, because many needs of people are immediate and urgent and demand my attention at that moment, not when it is convenient for me or my planned schedule.

Those are extreme illustrations, but many in the ministry fit into one of those categories or somewhere in between. A better and more biblical approach would be to look at my life and ministry though the lens of stewardship. We are temporal, and can only accomplish so much in this life. Jesus fulfilled all the will of God in His short thirty-three years. Realizing that we do not know how much time we have, and that our days are numbered, should motivate us to plan appropriately, so that the maximum amount of time and service can be given to fulfilling what God has called us to do.

One of the greatest hindrances to doing all the will of God for our lives is when we do not discipline the use of our limited time. There are priorities for ministers. Whatever your method of planning is, you must be careful to not violate God's order for your life. Paul addressed this in Timothy's life when he listed the qualifications for ministers in 1 Timothy 3:1–7. If you study that list you will quickly recognize that God is interested in the inner man that is then revealed in outward actions. You will notice that discipline and self-control are essential to fulfilling your mission on earth. Planning certainly fits into that motif.

Planning is simply a tool to enable you to use your time, gifts, and resources to their maximum capacity in order that you do not look back on a wasted life. Planning will force you to think and evaluate and get counsel and pray. Planning will ease the pressure in your life as a ministry—and a lack of planning will create stress and dissatisfaction. Planning will help you accomplish your ministry calling and will help you fulfill the qualifications for a minister. Planning helps overcome the natural tendency we all have to be lazy. Simply put, planning is essential in the life of a successful minister of the Gospel. Great tools and advice are available to us today. Let's not neglect this wonderful opportunity to buy up all the moments the Lord gives us and use them for His glory through appropriate planning.

Bob Graham
Pastor, Olathe View Baptist Church
Olathe, Kansas

WHEN I CONSIDER THE SUBJECT of planning, keeping track of the miscellaneous tasks that come our way tends to come to mind. We plan our work and work our plan, but other folks have plans they are working on as well, and sometimes their plans warrant our involvement and that can consume a fair amount of our time. Maintaining a master list of these tasks, with priorities and due dates, can prevent these items from falling between the cracks. But be careful not to allow the master list to turn into a procrastination device. There are some tasks that would be far better off never making it to our master list; attending to these tasks immediately may not only prove to be the most efficient means of handling the task, but also the most effective means of serving the one who brought it to our attention. For this reason, it might be wise to plan time in our daily schedules for unexpected activities.

One note of caution in this matter of planning and scheduling: Be careful how much of it you take home. Rigid planning and preoccupation with accomplishing tasks and goals often does little to build relationships. Our wives and our children are not impressed when they are reduced to an item on our "To-Do List." This is not to say that we don't have goals and objectives with regard to our relationships; we simply need to pursue them with a bit more savvy. Wise is the man who is able to be serious and spontaneous, productive and personal, and focused and still fun to be around.

"I KNOW SUNDAY'S BULLETIN IS HERE SOMEWHERE ON MY DESK!"

CHAPTER 7

THE CALL TO ORGANIZING

Ponder the path of thy feet, and let all thy ways be established.

Proverbs 4:26

Bringing into captivity every thought to the obedience of Christ.

2 Corinthians 10:5

Let us lay aside every weight, and the sin which doth so easily beset us,
and let us run with patience the race that is set before us.

Hebrews 12:1

HAVING CONSIDERED PLANNING, WHICH IS the envisioning of a project and its step-by-step accomplishment; we now want to look at organizing. Organizing deals with ways to approach your tasks to get more done, to do those tasks better and in less time. It is a general principle that applies to any project. The most successful people are not necessarily the smartest, but those who use their time best, setting goals and working toward those goals in an efficient manner.

Will Rogers used to say, "It's not so much what you do each

day; it's what you get done that counts." I learned this important principle when I was in management years ago. I was a young department manager, excited about what I was doing and willing to work long and hard. Then one day the district manager came to visit my department. Within a few minutes he found several things that needed to be changed. He pointed out old merchandise, poor buying habits, and markdowns that I had been too busy to make. I suppose that this wise executive saw the frustration on my face. He took the time to sit down with me and talk about organization. He told me that I needed to either conclude my day or begin my day by taking twenty minutes to design my next day. He listed three categories of things that fit into the day: things I *must do*, things I *should do*, and things I *would like to do*.

That wise counsel has paid off, not only in management but also in ministry. There are days when I have worked hard for long hours, but at the conclusion of the day, I have had almost all of the same tasks to accomplish as I had at the beginning of that day. There have been other days when I have organized myself, written down what needed to be done, and then begun to work from that To Do list. At the end of those days, I could look back and see what I had accomplished.

> BECAUSE THE APOSTLE PAUL WAS A MAN MASTERED BY A CAUSE, HE MASTERED HIMSELF.

We all have our interruptions and exceptions. Things come up that we had not planned. Still, organizing is the key to getting things done.

The Apostle Paul was a man who got things done. He was a

producer. Because he was a man mastered by a cause, he mastered himself. People buy books by motivational experts because they want to see how "successful people" got that way. The Bible gives many interesting details about the life of Paul. Look for a minute at these insights the Holy Spirit gives on the success strategy of this great individual.

A LOOK AT A SUCCESSFUL LEADER

> Know ye not that they which run in a race run all, but one receiveth the prize? So run, that ye may obtain. And every man that striveth for the mastery is temperate in all things. Now they do it to obtain a corruptible crown; but we an incorruptible. I therefore so run, not as uncertainly; so fight I, not as one that beateth the air: But I keep under my body, and bring it into subjection: lest that by any means, when I have preached to others, I myself should be a castaway. (1 Corinthians 9:24–27)

When Paul says, "So run, that ye may obtain" (v. 24), he implies that there are different ways to run this race. He says run *this way*—to gain the prize, to accomplish your goal. This is a vigorous passage, full of action words: "They which *run* . . . every man that *striveth* . . . I therefore so *run* . . . so *fight* I . . ." (emphasis mine). He is not just out there to make an entry in the fields of competition. He is out there to get a job done successfully!

In sports competition, you sometimes see the "loser's limp." A defending football player pursues the man with the ball down the field. As the man with the ball pulls ahead, the defender slows down sharply and hobbles to the sidelines. "Of course the poor boy couldn't catch him," the crowd is supposed to think. "He's injured." There is no loser's limp in Paul's race. He is in it to get the job done. Sure, he had problems and setbacks, but he kept giving it his all.

In verse 25, we are given a clue on the distinctive running style of the one who is serious: "Every man that striveth is *temperate* in all things." This is self-control. We must take full responsibility for using our time well. Temperance applies to matters of right and wrong; but it also applies to matters of good, better, and best.

In Hebrews 12:1, believers are told to "lay aside every weight" as well as "the sin which doth so easily beset us." There is a ring of certainty in Paul's voice in verse 26: "I therefore so run, not as uncertainly; so fight I, not as one that beateth the air." There are two outstanding characteristics of a successful person seen here. First, he has a job to do, he knows what it is, and he is going to stay on target until it gets done. Second, there is no half-hearted effort: he is not shadowboxing. He is not playing around at the ministry—he is dead earnest.

Finally, in verse 27, Paul addresses one of his great motivations. He does not want to be a castaway: "Lest that by any means, when I have preached to others, I myself should be a castaway." He wants his life to count. He does not want to be ashamed when he stands at the Judgment Seat of Christ.

Paul was definitely not strolling down the avenue of life in a lackadaisical way. If we want to be get-it-done people, we need to implement some organizational strategies in our personal lives and in our approach to the ministry. For many of us, poor habits of organization are weights that slow us down in the race of life. It is time to systematically lay aside our weights of poor organizational habits.

DAILY PERSONAL ORGANIZATION

Let's look at six things that you can do to organize your work for greater efficiency.

I. START WITH A CLEAN DESK

A desk cluttered with notes, memos, the morning mail, and all kinds of papers is a minefield that will destroy any sense of schedule. It is very easy to get sidetracked by some little project that just happens to catch your eye.

The first thing I try to do each morning is to organize my desk. I have a *To Do* stack. Things that I have not yet looked at go there. I will look through these things as time permits during the day. I also have a *Projects* stack. The projects that I will be working on are already on my To Do list for the day. Phone calls that I need to make or return are posted on a separate list. I get rid of as many pieces of paper as I can by placing messages on my To Do list or Phone Call list. In this age of electronic mail and other devices, we should clean up and delete information, organize our Outlook calendars, and make our technology work for us.

2. ORGANIZE YOUR DAY

Select today's work. Write down appointments, things you must do, and things you should do on a To Do Today list. Appointment books, pocket calendars, and electronic planners are great tools for this.

Be realistically demanding of yourself. Being realistic means that you are not going to build Rome before lunch. Being demanding means that you are going to structure your day to accomplish the To Do list.

3. WORK FROM THE TO DO LIST

Now that you have formulated this list, make it work for you. Take it seriously. Interruptions will come, and urgencies will break in. But with a clean desk and a To Do list, it is easy to get right back on schedule after the interruption.

4. MAKE PHONE CALLS AND ANSWER E-MAILS IN BLOCKS OF TIME

As much as possible, make your phone calls in one block of time. Lock in a thirty-minute period in midmorning to make all the calls on the Phone Call list. Set periods of time for checking electronic messages. If possible, turn off e-mail and other messaging alerts to avoid the distraction of a new message every couple of minutes. Those messages can usually wait until a predetermined time for handling messages.

5. PUT NEW PROJECTS IN THEIR PLACE

While you are working, other needs may develop. You might think of other things that need to be done, you might get messages alerting you of new needs. These are important, but they are rarely important enough that you should stop what you are doing. If we are not careful, our train of thought will be derailed by every whim and walnut shell that lies on the tracks.

Write these new projects down on the To Do list. If they must be done today, write them on the To Do Today list. This way you can get back to what you were working on. As you schedule your day, it is good to schedule some open time just for handling these emergencies. This way you can stay on schedule even with the unforeseen interruptions.

6. CROSS OUT ITEMS AS YOU GET THEM DONE

Cross out items on the weekly To Do list as you place them on your To Do Today list. Then cross out items on the To Do Today list as you get them done. Not only is this good for keeping track of what is done, but there is also a real sense of accomplishment as you see the items on your To Do Today list being done.

All of these things are essential to your management of your own time. They allow you to move at peace and at ease amidst the whirlwind of beseeching activities. Too often we are like the man in that classic mixed metaphor who "got on his horse and rode off in all directions at once."

> TOO OFTEN WE ARE LIKE THE MAN IN THAT CLASSIC MIXED METAPHOR WHO "GOT ON HIS HORSE AND RODE OFF IN ALL DIRECTIONS AT ONCE."

There are also procedures to make your interaction with other people and aspects of the ministry more effective. Let's consider these next.

ORGANIZING THE BIGGER PICTURE

SCHEDULE YOUR TIME

You must get some kind of planning device for appointments and for writing down notes to yourself on what must be done. There are many high-tech items available, but your device can be as simple as a pad and pencil (they don't run low on batteries, don't require download time, nor a lengthy series of clicks to locate the needed information). What works best for me is a little booklet that provides a calendar page for each day and a place to list all the things that need to be accomplished. Normally, I try to do this on Saturdays. There is not as much activity around the office, and I spend some time writing down all that must be done for the next week. I then begin to cross things off that list as I assign them to specific days, and sometimes even specific time frames during those days. Having this information in the same book as my appointments gives me the opportunity at the beginning of each day to write out what must be done, what the specific appointment times are that I am committed to, and what phone calls I need to make or e-mails I need to send. I have found that spending thirty minutes in planning at the beginning of each week is crucial to organization.

There are two important claims on our time. First of all is the Word of God. It is the eternal, unchanging, master blueprint for life. It deserves our time and attention. Second, we must make time for people. People are the key to our ministry; they are the reason for our ministry; they *are* the ministry. We must give our time to people.

ORGANIZE MINISTRY ACTIVITIES

Organizing your projects in the ministry is as important as organizing your own life. I like to plan well in advance. I look over the calendar to see what is coming up and what I need to be doing this week. If there is publicity that should be gotten out or if there are people whose help should be enlisted, I want to attend to these needs early. Many times a project that is on time is easy, whereas a project that is late is nearly impossible.

Writing things down, or entering them into whatever electronic device you use, is critical. It makes little difference how you do this; just write them down. Yellow legal pads are a simple, but good, way to get projects organized. Have one yellow pad for each project. Write the title of the project on the top of

> **ARE YOU OPERATING IN THE STRENGTH OF THE GIFTS THAT GOD HAS GIVEN YOU?**

the pad. Then, as you work on that project little by little, all of your ideas are kept together. This avoids the situation described on a certain bumper sticker: "I finally got my act together, but I forgot where I put it!"

MAXIMUM EFFECTIVENESS, MINIMUM WEARINESS

Are you operating in the strength of the gifts that God has given you? This principle, "maximum effectiveness with minimum weariness," is an important clue to the answer tothat question.

All of us have our strengths and weaknesses. When we operate in the area of our strengths—that is, in the area of our gifts—we perform at our maximum effectiveness with very little weariness involved. Other things take a lot of time, leave us worn out, and accomplish very little. The key is for all of us as staff members to get to know one another well enough to be a help to others in our areas of strength. We need to be humble enough, likewise, to seek help form others. We are a ministry team.

UTILIZATION OF SPIRITUAL GIFTS

In order to operate in the strengths God has given you, you must understand and practice your spiritual gifts. Understanding one's motivation in ministry promotes effectiveness. Do you understand the spiritual gifts as they are given in Romans 12:4–8 (motivational gifts), Ephesians 4:11–13, and 1 Corinthians 12:7–12? I encourage you to do a personal study on spiritual gifts as it relates to the ministry as a body of believers. Understand your gifts as you function as a staff. Teach this understanding to your lay leadership so that everyone seeks to minister as part of that body utilizing his or her gifts and strengths.

UNDERSTANDING SPIRITUAL GIFTS

And he gave some, apostles; and some, prophets; and some, evangelists; and some, pastors and teachers; For the perfecting of the saints, for the work of the ministry, for the edifying of the body of Christ; Till we all come in the unity of the faith, and of the knowledge of the Son of God, unto a perfect man, unto the measure of the stature of the fullness of Christ. Eph. 4:11–13

Of the three passages dealing most with spiritual gifts, the Ephesians 4 passage focuses most on the ministry use of gifts. Three basic truths make a starting place for application:

1. Everyone receives one or more spiritual gifts at salvation (Rom. 12:3).
2. As people use their spiritual gifts to serve, they experience great satisfaction and the effectiveness of their ministries is greatly enhanced (Eph. 4:12).
3. A leader's job is to train believers in the process of ministry. We are to perfect the saints to do the work of the ministry, so that the body might be edified (Ephesians 4:12).

ORGANIZING YOUR LIFE

You should not only schedule your weeks and your projects, but you should also schedule and monitor your own personal growth in light of your understanding of your spiritual gifts.

1. Identify various topics that you need to study for your personal growth and assign them to specific times each week. Systematically study a couple of these each week. Personally, I have spent a lot of time studying leadership, finances, and management. I try to read three books each month. These things help me to keep learning and growing. They keep me from getting stale.

2. Evaluate where you are in comparison to where you should be. Psalm 90 is one of the Bible's greatest statements on time. In verse 12, David asks God to help him keep a proper perspective on life: "So teach us to number our days, that we may apply our hearts unto wisdom." This kind of evaluation can spare you from many heartaches and many wasted years. Jacob wasted several years of his life because what he had done to his brother hindered his relationship with God. Are you on track in your spiritual growth, or are you in a holding pattern because of some roadblock in your spiritual development? To assist in this kind of evaluation, use a self-evaluation survey to direct your thoughts.

We should likewise evaluate our fulfillment of our responsibilities. The first thing that God gave to man in Genesis 2 was a responsibility. Responsibility is very important to all of us. We need to consider if we are responsibly handling the duties that are entrusted to us.

3. Have a balance in your life. Sometimes you need to say no to others for the sake of meeting your own personal needs. Sometimes

you need to say no to yourself to meet the needs of others. Both are equally important. We need to "gladly spend and be spent" (2 Corinthians 12:15). But there is no virtue in Christian burnout, either. This balance takes time and wisdom to attain, but it is very important.

4. Have a proper direction for your life, your family, and your ministry. In what condition do you want each of these areas to be one year from now? What steps will you have to take to get there? This goes back to goal setting. Life is like juggling: you have to keep several balls in the air. Organizing your life to give assigned time to consider yearly and weekly goals will help you master this juggling act.

5. List every role that you are presently fulfilling. Of these roles, list those that could be eliminated or delegated. Finally, list all the remaining roles that you should continue to have after the others are eliminated or delegated.

6. Prioritize the roles that you are keeping. Give each of them a place in your schedule.

PRIORITIES

We need to look at the use of our time the way God does. Listed in Ephesians 5 and 6 are what I call *God's priorities*. In these two chapters, Paul, under the inspiration of the Holy Spirit, goes right down the list of the major relationships in our lives. He starts in the logical place, our relationship to God.

Be ye therefore followers of God, as dear children. (Eph. 5:1)

Be filled with the Spirit. (v. 18)

Giving thanks always for all things unto God and the Father in the name of our Lord Jesus Christ. (v. 20)

PRIORITY #1: A PERSONAL RELATIONSHIP WITH GOD

These verses begin with the general statement, "Be ye therefore followers of God." Each member of the Trinity is then specifically mentioned. The message is clear: we need to start with God, "for of him, and through him, and to him, are all things" (Romans 11:36). If we are not right with God, we cannot hope to be right with others for very long. The key is to start out with a right relationship with the Lord; this will really assist us in having the right relationships with other people.

PRIORITY #2: THE RELATIONSHIP WITH A SPOUSE

After many comments about the elements of this right relationship to God, Paul goes on to the second great priority for many of us.

Submitting yourselves one to another in the fear of God. (Eph. 5:21)

Wives, submit yourselves unto your own husbands, as unto the Lord. (v. 22)

Husbands, love your wives, even as Christ also loved the church, and gave himself for it. (v. 25)

The Lord has given many of us a husband or wife. With that privilege comes a responsibility: that person becomes our number two priority. Paul spends almost as much of Chapter 5 on this relationship as he does on our relationship with God.

PRIORITY #3: THE RELATIONSHIP BETWEEN PARENTS AND CHILDREN

Of course, there are no chapter divisions in the original Greek. The text leads naturally into Chapter 6, verses 1–4:

Children, obey your parents in the Lord. (v. 1)

And, ye fathers, provoke not your children to wrath: but bring them up in the nurture and admonition of the Lord. (v. 4)

Like the husband-wife relationship, this one will definitely color all other relationships. If we neglect our children, a gloom will obscure the rest of our ministries, because "How can I go up to my father, and the lad be not with me?" (Genesis 44:34).

PRIORITY #4: RELATIONSHIPS BETWEEN STAFF MEMBERS

Without any transition, the text in Ephesians chapter 6 moves on to cover some of the key relationships in our world of work:

Servants, be obedient to them that are your masters according to the flesh, with fear and trembling, in singleness of your heart, as unto Christ. (v. 5)

And, ye masters, do the same things unto them, forbearing threatening: knowing that your Master also is in heaven; neither is there respect of persons with him. (v. 9)

This is a tremendous study! I call it "internal staff ethics." In Ephesians 6:5–9, Paul presents general principles of how we, as subordinates, should relate to those over us. It also deals with our role as superior to those who are our subordinates. It tells us that we are all to be servants, to serve one another as if we were serving the Lord Himself.

Our ministries are *ministries*, but they are also our paid employment. We should be as determined to accomplish something worthwhile as someone who is merely seeking fame and fortune for himself. We are striving to please God, not to win the applause of men. But you must truly *strive* to do a work for God.

Thus far we have addressed four big roles:

- God
- Spouse
- Children
- Work associates

PRIORITY #5: OUR RESPONSIBILITY TO MINISTER TO OTHERS

In Ephesians 6:10–17, Paul describes the preparation for this ministry in terms of the armor of the Christian. Then in verses 18 and 19 he refers to some specific actions of ministry: "Praying . . . for all saints; And for me . . . that I may open my mouth boldly, to make known the mystery of the gospel."

This section does not deal with all possible aspects of ministry, but it does deal with representative examples from the two broad groups to whom we minister.

First, we minister to Christians. Paul asks for prayer for the believers and for himself in particular. He doesn't ask for encouragement, or hospitality, or the meeting of financial needs. All of these are important, and all of these are addressed elsewhere. However, after describing the Christian's armor and referring to the terrible forces against which he knew his fellow believers were in mortal conflict, "principalities . . . powers . . . the rulers of the darkness of this world," Paul exhorts them to pray. We learn from this that there really is not a contrast between "doing something practical" for a brother or sister in Christ and "just praying." Praying is one of the most practical things we can do.

Second, we reach out to non-Christians. Paul refers to his own outreach ministry. He stands as an example to the Ephesian believers in his bold outreach to the lost.

Our responsibilities extend beyond the paid position, beyond the classroom or office walls. If we do not take time for ministry beyond what we are paid to do, we will shrivel into spiritual prunes.

It is one thing to fail because we tried to do something that we were unable to do. It is quite another thing to fail because we were not paying attention, because we just did not notice the daily erosion of our responsibility.

Along the south shore of Lake Erie, the water laps against the high bluffs year after year. Every couple of years the newspapers will have a picture of a house that has tumbled twenty or thirty feet into the lake. Because the owners did not pay attention to the little, gradual changes, the calamity came. And when it came, it came suddenly, irreversibly.

To avoid being caught unaware like that, we need to organize our lives to balance our priorities.

***

Life Principle:

Let your purpose prioritize your life. Philippians 2:3–8

FURTHER REFLECTIONS

Bruce McAllister★
Director of Ministerial Training and Extension, Bob Jones University
Greenville, SC

★Mr. McAllister has graciously allowed me to reproduce an article he wrote for Today's Christian Preacher, *Summer 2007, to further illustrate the content of this chapter.*

SETTING PRIORITIES & BEING PRODUCTIVE

Instead of trying to do the work of 20 people, develop 20 people to do the work.

THE PASTOR IS THE "STEWARD of God" (Titus 1:7). He is the household manager serving the Lord's interests in His church while He is away. When the Lord returns, He will call the pastor into account for how faithfully he managed the local church (1 Peter 5:4; Hebrews 13:17; 1 Corinthians 4:1–5). What does it mean to be a faithful steward? Jesus' parables in Luke's gospel define the faithful steward. He is active at his task (Luke 12:42–48), attentive to detail (Luke 16:1–12) and productive in profit making (Luke 19:12–27).

The pastor should take all his God-given resources and turn a spiritual profit for the kingdom and glory of God. Those resources include the Word of God; the Holy Spirit's power; prayer; and his and others' time, money, facilities, equipment, talents and spiritual gifts. God wants men of integrity and industry who will carry out their tasks with energy, enthusiasm and endurance. He wants them to be trustworthy and faithful. To meet all those qualifications, a pastor must set priorities and be productive. Begin to evaluate your faithful stewardship by asking the following questions:

Am I genuinely right with God and walking in fellowship with Him?

God promises to cause a man's activities to prosper when he meditates day and night in the Word of God (Psalm 1:1–3; Joshua 1:8). Sometimes pastors stray from God, become self-willed and self-centered, and forget that they are stewards of what God has given them. When personal discipline falters, effective ministry suffers. In his book *The Preacher: His Life and Work,* John Henry Jowett wrote: "I am profoundly convinced that one of the gravest perils which besets the ministry of this country is a restless scattering of energies over an amazing multiplicity of interests, which leaves no margin of time or of strength for receptive and absorbing communion with God. . . . We must, therefore, hold firmly and steadily to this primary principle, that of all things that need doing, this need is supreme, to live in intimate fellowship with God."[2]

Have I clearly defined my primary ministry goals and tasks?

The local church is a community evangelistic base and discipling agency. The Great Commission is fulfilled through a local church ministry as the pastor equips and leads his people to evangelize sinners and disciple believers. The pastor should have a plan for contacting every home in the community for Christ. He should have a specific plan for personal or group discipleship and relationship building.

---

2   John Henry Jowett, *The Preacher, His Life and Work* (New York; London: Harper & Brothers, 1912), 62–63.

Am I maximizing the use of my time toward accomplishing primary ministry goals and tasks?

John Henry Jowett wrote: "Enter your study at an appointed hour, and let that hour be as early as the earliest of your businessmen goes to his warehouse or his office. . . . Let him [the pastor] employ system and method, and let him be as scrupulously punctual in the service of his Lord. . . . Let him estimate the comparative values of things. Let first things be put first, and let him give the freshness of his strength to matters of vital and primary concern."[3]

Consider the following six questions regarding time management:

1. *Am I utilizing time blocks of focused effort on specific projects and excluding all non-emergency intrusions?* The demands of preparing to preach and teach require blocks of study time throughout the week. If you preach three times a week, you should plan to study 15 to 20 hours. Mornings are probably the best time since your people are working at their jobs. Limit distractions and keep the focus on study and prayer. Have your office manager or wife screen calls, convey messages, prepare bulletins and check on purchases. Use blocks of afternoon time for church business, counseling, visitation, and developing ministry projects and programs.

2. *Am I taking time to plan and prioritize in advance the use of my week or month, and am I sticking to the plan?* Prioritizing one's plan of activities takes time. Much greater productivity and satisfaction result from careful forethought. The guiding question for prioritizing is: "What difference will

---

3   Ibid., 116–117.

doing this task make?" The greater the difference, the more important the task.

3. *Am I staying disciplined, following a weekly schedule and daily planner?* You should have a written and/or electronic weekly schedule, and only true emergencies should deter you from working that plan. Don't waste your time reading junk mail, listening to talk radio at the office, taking long coffee or lunch breaks at local restaurants, talking on the phone with no ministry purpose, or spending too much time on blogs and other Internet sites. Also, be sure to communicate tactfully your priorities to the congregation so that they will not misunderstand your good intentions.

4. *Am I allowing 10 percent of my people to dominate 90 percent of my ministry time?* Certain people tend to demand an inordinate amount of a pastor's time. While compassion reaches out to them, compassion must curtail the time those people seek in order to allow time for others in the church or community as well.

5. *Am I using the best tools to maximize productivity?* Read only the best expositional commentaries. Don't waste time reading verbose, obtuse authors. In addition, today's Bible software programs for computers allow you to do rapid word studies and searches that previously would have taken hours. Make good use of your driving time by listening to informative or inspirational sermons or ministry-related CDs.

6. *Am I saving time by effectively managing ministry information?* The most important information should be immediately accessible at your desk and in your day planner, PDA, computer

and car. Maintain reference information about the church's programs, people, scheduling, pressing projects and church policies. If you are not skilled at setting up an information management system, enlist the help of a capable office manager.

Are my body and mind operating at peak performance?

A pastor carries out his ministry within the limitations of a human body and mind. Too many pastors follow a sedentary lifestyle, which denies them the energy and vigor they could have. How easy it is to unconsciously seek more energy through constant snacking, overeating and frequent napping when what is truly needed is a healthy diet and routine exercise. Brisk walking, jogging, swimming and other forms of aerobic exercise increase physical stamina and mental alertness. Pastors who take their example from Paul should consider how often he must have walked 20 miles in a day!

Am I building and developing people?

Instead of trying to do the work of 20 people, develop 20 people to do the work. Paul spent time developing co-laborers like Timothy, Titus, Tychicus, Epaphroditus, Epaphras, Aquila and Priscilla. He relied on those people to carry out and expand the ministry. Build people through effective preaching and teaching and by spending productive personal time with them. Convey your burden and communicate your priorities. Personally enlist their help on ministry projects. Using these techniques and answering these questions will help you gain the maximum spiritual profit for our Lord's kingdom.

CHAPTER 8

THE CALL TO LEADING

My brethren, be not many masters, knowing that we shall receive the greater condemnation [the stricter accountability].

James 3:1

And whosoever will be chief among you, let him be your servant:
Even as the Son of man came not to be ministered unto, but to minister,
and to give his life a ransom for many.

Matthew 20:27–28

Let the elders that rule well be counted worthy of double honour,
especially they who labour in the word and doctrine.

1 Timothy 5:17

HAVE YOU HEARD THE STORY about the soldier on patrol? He was deep within enemy territory when he radioed back to his sergeant, "I've just captured a large company of prisoners!"

"Great," replied the sergeant, "Bring them in."

"They won't come, Sarge."

"Then you come back."

"They won't let me!"

This soldier's control of the situation was questionable, at best. It is one thing to say that you are a leader; but if no one is following, you are not leading and not much will get done.

WHAT IS LEADERSHIP?

Are some people born leaders? In some sense, yes. This simply means that early in life they developed certain skills and personality traits. "Made leaders" develop these same skills and traits later in life. If God has called you to serve in a ministry, you should conscientiously develop these skills for maximum effectiveness. This is true for the born leader as well as for one who senses real needs and is striving to grow in this area.

> **EVERY PERSON IS A LEADER TO SOMEONE.**

Yet, in a very real way, every person is a leader to someone. Each of us influences others, for better or for worse. Even an example of noninvolvement has potential to lead others to the same thing. Again, this makes it a high priority that we understand the process of leadership and make it work effectively for us in our service for the Lord.

LEADERSHIP AS DIRECTION

Leadership is the process of providing direction. It is more than guidance though. The leader is also the one who provides motivation: he makes things happen. He is the engine, not just the steering wheel.

In any organization or group that I have ever been affiliated with, I have found three groups of people. First, there are those who do not know what is happening. They are there and they are part of the group, but they really have no idea what is going on. Second, there are those who watch what is happening. While they may understand the purpose and take some small part in the function, they do not get very much involved. Third, there are those who cause what is happening. This is the small minority that becomes the leaders of the group. All you have to do is attend an athletic event to observe all three categories in action.

LEADERSHIP AS INFLUENCE

Leadership can best be described as *influence*. The Lord Jesus Christ spent a large part of the Sermon on the Mount analyzing this aspect of leadership. We see in Matthew 5:13–15 two analogies He used to do it:

1. Salt: "Ye are the salt of the earth: but if the salt have lost his savour, wherewith shall it be salted? it is thenceforth good for nothing, but to be cast out, and to be trodden under foot of men."

2. Light: "Ye are the light of the world. A city that is set on an hill cannot be hid. Neither do men light a candle, and put it under a bushel, but on a candlestick; and it giveth light unto all that are in the house."

We are the "salt of the earth." First, Christianity gives flavor to life, Christianity is a superior way of life. The "seasoning" of love, joy, and peace is extremely attractive to the lost person whose senses are dulled by sins and excesses. Second, salt preserves. We stand for right in an age of wrong. We preserve the right ways which, even among less-corrupt lost people, have a natural savor of right because of "the law written in their hearts" (Romans 2:14–15). Third, salt heals. When people see relationships, marriages, and lives healed by the consistent application of biblical principles of living, they take notice. And, finally, salt also creates thirst. When people see all of these things taking place, their hope is renewed that life can have purpose and joy. Thoreau accurately wrote that "most men live lives of quiet desperation," but the example of a Christian's life sets in motion a divine thirst designed to draw the lost to the water of life.

We are also "light": individually, candles; collectively, a whole city of lights. We are to illuminate the path and show people the way to God.

All of these images—salt, candles, the city on a hill—portray influence. This means that we are called to leadership. It is not that only paid staff members are to be leaders in these senses, but all Christians are. As staff, however, we are to be examples to our people. We, of all Christians, should be salt and light.

TYPES OF LEADERSHIP

We have all seen situations where one person was the official leader, but someone else was the one who really ran the show. A certain humorous "corporate organizational chart" has a box labeled this way: "secretary (secretly runs the whole shootin' match)." It takes more than a brass nameplate to be a leader. You would do well to understand where you are and where you need to be growing in the four kinds of leadership.

POSITIONAL LEADERSHIP

By position alone, someone may be a leader. He or she is the official, recognized director: the person in charge, the manager, "The Boss." Paul addresses this type of leadership in Romans 13:1–2: "Let every soul be subject unto the higher powers. For there is no power but of God: the powers that be are ordained of God. Whosoever therefore resisteth the power, resisteth the ordinance of God: and they that resist shall receive to themselves damnation."

This type of leadership most certainly counts. It comes with divine sanction. But this is not the only type of leadership. A title does not make a person a good leader; but, ideally, good leaders will end up being the ones with the position.

COMPETENT LEADERSHIP

People who are good at what they do—and willing to work hard at it—tend to stand out. They are the ones who are "redeeming the time, because the days are evil" (Ephesians 5:16).

With or without the title, people soon learn who to look to when a job needs to be done. For instance, if I need work done on my car, I should go to someone who knows something about auto mechanics. He is the authority in this situation. I would certainly rather have the competence without a title than have a title without any expertise.

PERSONALITY LEADERSHIP

Sometimes people become leaders because others enjoy being around them. There are certain people that we enjoy being with, and when they make a sugges-

> **LEADERSHIP BY EXAMPLE IS THE BEST KIND OF LEADERSHIP.**

tion, it is normally easy to follow them because we like them. These are the ones who evidence the fruits of Galatians 5:22–23: "But the fruit of the Spirit is love, joy, peace, longsuffering, gentleness, goodness, faith, meekness, temperance: against such there is no law."

Observe a group of people interacting freely, as at a church fellowship or a teen activity. It does not take long to figure out who these personality leaders are. Listen to radio talk show hosts. They speak with firmness, an earnest solicitousness, and a confidence that—rightly or wrongly—inspires their listener to believe in their words, and they influence millions.

CHARACTER LEADERSHIP

However, over all of these, the best kind of leadership is leadership by example; in other words, leadership by character. Paul directed words on leadership to his young son in the ministry, Timothy: "Let no man despise thy youth; but be thou an example of the believers, in word, in conversation, in charity, in spirit, in faith, in purity" (1 Timothy 4:12). The best leaders model the skills and attitudes necessary for their followers' success. A good sales manager sells. A good school administrator organizes and has the ability to teach. And a good pastor has a pure life and wins souls.

A person is a leader to the extent he manifests any one of these leadership traits, but the most effective leader will develop all of them. He will especially work on the last: leading by "do as I do." In light of that, no one has "arrived" as a leader. We all have room to grow.

In 1 Kings 12, we read of a failure of leadership. After the death of Solomon, the people of this young kingdom came to the new king, Rehoboam, with a pretty reasonable set of demands: the kingdom is set up; the palace and the temple are built; let up the taxes and we will gladly follow you. The older counselors told Rehoboam, "Grant their request and you will win their allegiance."

If Rehoboam had been an example, had manifested the right character, and had listened to the people and served them, they would have served him forever. "If thou wilt be a servant unto this people this day, and wilt serve them, and answer them, and speak good words to them, then they will be thy servants for ever" (1 Kings 12:7).

But Rehoboam listened to the advice of his peers—lazy products of luxurious court life, men who had no idea of what had gone into the making of the kingdom. He adopted a tough attitude that was oriented toward exalting himself. As a result, he tore a kingdom in two—and he ended up with a small piece.

In all of these kinds of leadership—positional, competent, personality, and character—we need to keep in mind that the gift of leadership has more responsibilities than privileges. Our goal is to make our followers happy and successful in their service to God. When we have done that, then—and only then—we will be happy and successful in our leadership.

THE PROCESS OF LEADERSHIP

Whatever types of leadership you possess, there are processes that work and processes that do not work. A simple formula can be your reminder for success—the I DO formula:

Initiate

Delegate

Oversee

Initiate

As a leader, you need to be the kind of individual who makes things happen. You must be a problem solver, not just a problem finder. Anyone can find problems, but finding the problem and its solution is the role of leadership. You and your ministry will grow together that way.

My job description has been filled with many different responsibilities over the years, from overseeing the Sunday school, being in charge of the adult ministry, heading up the lay ministry programs within our church, and on and on the list goes. None of these is what I was called to do when I entered the ministry. They were simply things that were not being done, and I began trying to solve problems. Just recently we have seen the need to have more opportunities for small group fellowship within our church. As our ministry has grown, it has become increasingly difficult for our people to get to know each other in a close, intimate way. As a possible solution, I proposed the initiation of Care/Share groups. These are monthly home Bible studies for people living in a certain geographical area. Guess who had the job of organizing and developing these? I do not mind. In fact, I love it, because it meets a need—and that is really what God has called me to do. I have been excited about the results: people caring for and sharing with one another in a greater way.

DELEGATE

It is important to see needs and to initiate solutions, but you cannot do everything yourself—nor should you. Properly managed delegation is good for you, for your work, and for those to whom you delegate.

Remember the advice given to Moses by his father-in-law, Jethro? He told Moses to divide the decision-making authority and the responsibility, delegating much of it to trustworthy men. These people then would judge all of the routine cases, but the hard matters would be brought to Moses. They would make Moses' load lighter by sharing it with him.

THE BENEFITS OF DELEGATION

As mentioned briefly in an earlier chapter, effective delegation is a good thing for everyone involved. Delegation gives you, as a leader, more time for your personal spiritual development. It allows you to deepen your ministry. This is the purpose of deacons. The apostles met with the Christians of that early church and said, "It is not reason that we should leave the word of God, and serve tables." They told the people to select seven men to administrate certain tasks, "but we will give ourselves continually to prayer, and to the ministry of the word" (Acts 6:2–4).

You must be careful that you do not grow so busy in the work that you lose your own perspective on spiritual things. This is happening throughout Christianity, today more than ever. We as leaders must have spiritual input, too.

Delegation is also valuable for the ones to whom you have entrusted certain tasks. It allows them to grow within the organization. It is very difficult to keep good men when they are not given responsibilities and some authority. If they never are more than detail people, they will not stay in the ministry long. Delegation stimulates employees to motivation and to commitment to the organization.

THE PROCESS OF DELEGATION

Recognize the limits of your capacity. No one can do everything well. We are a body, and each member needs the other members. Not only that, but each member needs to be needed. One clue to recognizing your special gifts is the "maximum effectiveness, minimum weariness" factor. What tasks do you perform very effectively, but they do not tire you? These are yours.

Select the projects or tasks to be delegated. Not everything is equally open for delegation. Your guideline is always, "What will better accomplish the furthering of the entire ministry?" Recognize also that every job has some negative elements in it. There will always be elements of your work that you have to keep if you are to keep the other associated elements that you get excited about.

Select the person best qualified to handle the responsibility. This person should be someone who would like to do it and seems to be good at that responsibility. You are finding someone who has maximum effectiveness with minimum weariness at the task.

Meet with that person to explain the task. Write out the important elements of this, including who, what, when, and where. Put down on paper a method of reporting back to you in progress and upon completion. This written instruction is very important, because we forget so much of what we hear. You have chosen a capable person whom you trust to creatively work through the assignment, but anything that must be done in a certain way must be written down.

Maintain accountability. You cannot delegate and forget. Periodically check up and be sure that progress is being made. This prevents surprises and it reinforces your availability to help.

OVERSEE

After initiating and delegating, we need to oversee. Make certain that everything for which you are responsible is being accomplished as it should be, when it should be. Good communication is a key to staff relations and the furtherance of the ministry.

For this oversight function, you need a system. There should be a systematic way of checking up on each project and ministry. You could use a simple yellow legal pad, 3x5 cards, or one of the number of electronic systems on the market today. Just do it! Keep in touch with all of the ministries for which you are accountable.

Initiate, delegate, oversee—these are the keys to reproducing your ministry through the lives of others and accomplishing the greatest good with the gifts God has given you.

CARING: THE E-N-D PRINCIPLE

The Apostle Paul had a very effective ministry. He set up church after church, and he continually checked back with them, directing and praying for them. The Holy Spirit opened the door of Paul's life and let a ray of sunlight fall on the heart of this great leader. This insight comes out in elements that God led Paul to write to the Thessalonians as he reflected back on his brief time among them.

First, he was an *example* to them: "For our gospel came not unto you in word only, but also in power, and in the Holy Ghost, and in much assurance; as ye know what manner of men we were among you for your sake. And ye became followers of us, and of the Lord" (1 Thessalonians 1:5–6). Paul and his team lived in a certain manner for the sake of these people they wanted to reach. Their love altered their lifestyle.

Second, Paul loved and *nurtured* the people: "But we were gentle among you, even as a nurse cherisheth her children: So being affectionately desirous of you, we were willing to have imparted unto you, not the gospel of God only, but also our own souls, because ye were dear unto us" (1 Thessalonians 2:7–8). He compared himself to a nursing mother in his tender care for these people. There is a depth of tenderness here. His compassion must have shown.

Third, after being an example to them and after loving them, Paul gave *direction*:

"As ye know how we exhorted and comforted and charged every one of you, as a father doth his children" (1 Thessalonians 2:11).

Many times pastors, principals, teachers, or administrators try to give direction to young people or those under them; but they have not been shown a consistent example and a consistent love. The END principle should be applied: there must be an *example* and *nurturing* in order to have effective *direction*. People will respond to our direction as they see the other two ingredients in our lives. It has been my observation over the years that people really want direction, even when they are reluctant to admit that they want it. We often teach more by what we are than by what we say. Effective leadership is largely a matter of loving your people.

MODEL-MOTIVATE-MENTOR

Over the years, I have expanded the END principle to what I now call Model-Motivate-Mentor—The Formula for Maximum Impact. In 1 Thessalonians 2, Paul gives a tremendous formula for leadership, described above as the END principle. The words *Model, Motivate,* and *Mentor,* however, suggest other aspects of Paul's method of ministry.

MODEL

Let us take a look first of all at our example, or modeling. People are impacted by what they see. This is one aspect of integrity, one's internal character open to outward scrutiny.

Continuation: "For yourselves, brethren, know our entrance in unto you, that it was not in vain: But even after that we had suffered before, and were shamefully entreated, as ye know, at Philippi, we were bold in our God to speak unto you the gospel of God with much contention" (1 Thessalonians 2:1–2). Paul was a never-quit kind of leader. Even after he had been mistreated in Philippi, he continued on.

Character: "For our exhortation was not of deceit, nor of uncleanness, nor in guile" (v. 3). Paul showed character in his manner of ministry, in his message of truth, and in his motive marked by purity.

Consistency: "But as we were allowed of God to be put in trust with the gospel, even so we speak; not as pleasing men, but God, which trieth our hearts. For neither at any time used we flattering words, as ye know, nor a cloke of covetousness; God is witness: Nor of men sought we glory, neither of you, nor yet of others, when we might have been burdensome, as the apostles of Christ" (v. 4–6). Paul's methods were not trickery. His modeling developed trust among the people, and trust brings about influence.

MOTIVATE

In 1 Thessalonians 2:7–9 we see how Paul motivated people by nurturing them. You can model the Christian life in a group, but to nurture someone, you have to work individually with him or her.

Gentleness: "But we were gentle among you, even as a nurse cherisheth her children" (v. 7). Paul was saying there was a gentleness in working with people. He compared it to a gentleness of a mother with a nursing baby. One way that gentleness is seen is in your patience in dealing with people who are in your spiritual care or under your leadership.

Affection: "So being affectionately desirous of you, we were willing to have imparted unto you, not the gospel of God only, but also our own souls, because ye were dear unto us" (v. 8). Love requires sacrificing yourself for the success of someone else. In 2 Corinthians 12:15, Paul said, "I will very gladly spend and be spent for you; though the more abundantly I love you, the less I be loved." This is loving others—sometimes when we do not even feel like it.

Devotion: "For ye remember, brethren, our labour and travail: for labouring night and day, because we would not be chargeable unto any of you, we preached unto you the gospel of God" (v. 9). People don't care how much you know until they know how much you care.

Take a moment to evaluate how you nurture those in your sphere of influence:

- Whom are you nurturing?
- Does this nurturing process extend itself to those in your home?
- What about on the job, in your neighborhood, and in your church?

God calls each of us to spiritual leadership, which involves the loving nurture of others. How is this done? First, we must commit ourselves to others. Second, we must be accessible to them. Third, we must give them opportunities for Christian growth and ministry. As a result we lift them to a higher level. This type of commitment, based on unselfish love, will motivate people to spiritual growth and to Christian service.

MENTOR

Paul's work: "For ye remember, brethren, our labour and travail: for laboring night and day, because we would not be chargeable unto any of you, we preached unto you the gospel of God" (v. 9). Paul was a hard-working person. In the context of this verse, we see that one reason for his diligence was that he wanted to earn the right to lead.

Paul's walk: "Ye are witnesses, and God also, how holily and justly and unblameably we behaved ourselves among you that believe" (v. 10). Paul was keenly aware that his lifestyle must be blameless if he was to lead these new believers into spiritual maturity. He allowed no hidden pockets of sin in his life.

Paul's words: "As ye know how we exhorted and comforted and charged every one of you, as a father doth his children, that ye would walk worthy of God, who hath called you unto his kingdom and glory" (vv. 11–12). Our words are powerful tools for spiritual leadership. Consider the three goals of Paul's words:

- To exhort—This involves two ideas: to call to one's side and to encourage. Paul was more than accessible; he was seeking to build relationships in order to build people.
- To comfort—This means to encourage to activity. It's not just making people *feel* better; it's helping them to *do* better.
- To charge—The idea here is to testify or to give personal witness to other people. To "charge" people whom you are mentoring, focus on their strengths. Then enlarge them through attitude, relationship, and leadership. Finally, expose them to other influences which will help them grow.

This process is key to leadership. It worked for Paul and it will work for you as well.

THREE PEOPLE

I have often heard Dr. Les Ollila, one of my mentors, state that every person needs three people in his life: He needs a Paul—someone he is learning from; he needs a Pal—someone he is accountable to, an iron-sharpening-iron friend; and he needs a Project—someone he is investing his life in.

A SUCCESS STORY

We find a heartwarming description of what can result from this Model-Motivate-Mentor process in Philippians 2:19–22:

> I trust in the Lord Jesus to send Timotheus shortly unto you, that I also may be of good comfort, when I know your state. For I have no man likeminded, who will naturally care for your state. For all seek their own, not the things which are Jesus Christ's. But ye know the proof of him, that, as a son with the father, he hath served with me in the gospel.

Let's look at what Paul was telling the people at Philippi. Paul hoped to get back to their church soon, but if he could not get back to them, he would send Timothy. Sending Timothy was just like Paul's being with them himself because Timothy was likeminded with Paul. Timothy was a consistent model of biblical living. He would naturally care for these people, even when others would be seeking their own personal benefit. Ministry was the motivating factor of Timothy's life. This all resulted from the time in which Timothy served alongside Paul. Paul mentored Timothy all that time, with the result that Timothy was mature and ready for greater challenges. This is our privilege and responsibility: to model the Christian life, to motivate our people through nurturing love, and finally, to mentor with the result of direction for Christian growth and service.

***

Life Principle:

Be a model, motivator, and mentor to others. IThess. 2:1–12

FURTHER REFLECTIONS

John Judson
Pastor, Gateway Baptist Church
Ketchikan, Alaska

THERE ARE TWO PRINCIPLES THAT I look for in leaders and that I strive to live by myself. This is based on the fact that I am what I am (1 Corinthians 15:10), and that what I am is okay. I have always taught that we are each a unique work of art, a vessel, prepared by our Lord to do a specific thing. God has taken my physical attributes as well as my talents and added teaching to create a blend that only he can use for any good. Add to that experiences, some of which I am ashamed of and some of which were very problematic, as well as those experiences that were great successes, and you have *me.*

The first of my defining principles I learned while an unsaved soldier at Fort Richardson, Alaska. The NCO academy had as its motto, "Lead by example." I've never forgotten that I cannot expect anyone around me, for any extended period of time, to do as I say and not as I do. This has everything to do with morale as well. Being one of these unfortunate individuals who wears his feelings on his sleeve, everyone knows when I am down or worried or anxious. If I want my people to be cheery, it doesn't do much good to bark at them to be happy! If I want my guys not to worry, it's hard to get that message across between the tears. For any policy or program or even doctrine or ministry, I must set the bar by doing and not simply by ordering.

The other principle that has transformed my life and become the driving force in my leadership is one that I learned 17 years after I had gotten saved, while at Bible school. I am not a well-educated man who has thought through many a deep subject, but this one I hang my hat on and demand of the folks around me: Do right. It's the simplest thing in the world, but I also feel it's the most important. It is unfortunate that men of God live in an aquarium, so to speak, where those around them look at their lives from the top, sides, and even the bottom up. But it's true. And I feel it is imperative that in all circumstances they see us do right. Especially when we've done wrong, our folks must see us make things right at the earliest possible opportunity.

The Apostle Paul never let his past prevent him from doing something presently. He was always willing and able before the Lord to say, "Follow me. Do as I'm doing." And he always insisted that his mentees do what was right before the Lord. The Lord has been gracious to put these two principles before me—one as an unsaved G.I., and one as an aspiring pastor. Combined with all the experiences of my life, and that God is the One who cleaned me up and made me fit for duty, it's just possible that something may be done for the glory of God.

CHAPTER 9

THE CALL TO EVALUATING

And Moses did look upon all the work, and, behold,

they had done it as the LORD had commanded,

even so had they done it: and Moses blessed them.

Exodus 39:43

Obey them that have the rule over you, and submit yourselves:

for they watch for your souls, as they that must give account, that they may

do it with joy, and not with grief: for that is unprofitable for you.

Hebrews 13:17

Yet have I sent the brethren, lest our boasting of you should be in vain in this behalf;

that, as I said, ye may be ready:

Lest haply if they of Macedonia come with me,

and find you unprepared, we (that we say not, ye) should be ashamed

in this same confident boasting.

2 Corinthians 9:3–4

I REALLY DO NOT KNOW how any of us survived the early years of my ministry at Tri-City. As youth leader and director of our inner-city bus ministry, I had teenagers visiting door-to-door in a government-supported, high-rise housing project. I found out later that repairmen would not go into that project without a police escort.

Beat the Devil Sunday is another experience I look back on with a smile and a groan. On Saturday, I had teens dressed up in devils' costumes, riding around the area surrounding the church in the back of a couple pickup trucks. They carried signs that read, "DON'T go to Tri-City Baptist Church on this Sunday." Some of the more mature people in the church were sitting back thinking, "That Matt Williams—he sure is zealous, but he sure is strange!" In evaluating my ministry over the years, I do believe there is more of a balanced approach today than there was in those days.

Perhaps there is a key point of balance here for you, too. Evaluation can help you keep the zeal while you gain the maturity. Maybe, as you consider God's call to evaluate your work and the work of others, there will be some things that you can grow in—I hope so. Even the

> WHERE THERE MAY BE EXCESSES FROM WELL-INTENTIONED ZEAL, OR EVEN FAILURES FROM PERSONAL WEAKNESSES, IT IS GOD'S PLAN THAT WE SHOULD EXAMINE THESE AREAS, GROW IN GRACE, AND "PRESS TOWARD THE MARK . . ."

Apostle Paul said, "Not as though I had already attained"; but he kept striving toward the goal of serving the Lord better (Philippians 3:12). In your work or in ministries that you are called to lead, there may be areas that you will look at and shake your head in wonder.

That is all right. Where there may be excesses from well-intentioned zeal, or even failures from personal weaknesses, it is God's plan that we should examine these areas, grow in grace, and "press toward the mark for the prize of the high calling of God in Christ Jesus" (Philippians 3:14).

AN EXAMPLE

In Luke 10 we see the Lord planning, organizing, leading, and evaluating a very extensive campaign. Let's look at the steps: "After these things the Lord appointed other seventy also, and sent them two and two before his face into every city and place, whither he himself would come" (v.1).

The Lord planned and organized His campaign. Knowing He had a limited amount of time, He placed certain cities on His must-visit list. He also selected individuals to go to those cities ahead of Him.

Then the Lord led the campaign. What we see in verses 2–16 is a training session. He warns and encourages His "staff." He covers every option: what if they are open to your message, and what if they are not; what should you take, and how will your needs be provided?

Finally, verses 17–24 give some insights into an evaluative session He had with these seventy disciples. He let them report: "And the seventy returned again with joy, saying, Lord, even the devils are subject unto us through thy name" (v.17).

Then the Lord shared with the disciples His observations—His evaluation—and He affirmed their worth:

And He said unto them, I beheld Satan as lightning fall from heaven.

Behold, I give unto you power to tread on serpents and scorpions, and over all the power of the enemy: and nothing shall by any means hurt you.

Notwithstanding in this rejoice not, that the spirits are subject unto you; but rather rejoice, because your names are written in heaven (vv. 18–20).

These disciples were excited when they got back. Even though Christ was going to correct a potential problem in their perspective, He started with a positive. He let them report their work. He not only praised their work, but also He reaffirmed that their worth to Him was not just in what they did, but in the love He had for them as individuals.

But He did very clearly correct their wrong perspective. The Lord told them not to be so excited about the sensational aspects of their ministry, their power over the spirit world. They needed to keep

> THE LORD JESUS PRAISED HIS PEOPLE; THEN HE WENT ON TO DEFLECT GLORY FROM HIMSELF TO GOD THE FATHER

their focus on the source of that power, their relationship to God. Yet, even this correction ended with a very positive element: "Your names are written in heaven."

In summary, we see praise, correction, and affirmation. The Lord Jesus praised His people; then He went on to deflect glory from Himself to God the Father: "In that same hour Jesus rejoiced in spirit, and said, I thank thee, O Father" (v. 21).

Notice that He "rejoiced in spirit." He let His disciples see His emotional side. He was not a marble-monument leader, above human emotion. His disciples knew how He felt about their actions. They knew when they had erred, too. The Lord was known for His stern rebuke as well as for His loving affirmation. Peter must have felt very uncomfortable when the Lord said, "Get thee behind me, Satan . . . thou savourest not the things that be of God" (Matthew 16:23).

Evaluation is a necessary step. Make sure that you include it.

THE NEED FOR EVALUATION

The need for evaluating is obvious, isn't it? Then why is it the most neglected part of leadership? I enjoy that old Chinese proverb that says, "You fool me once, shame on you. You fool me twice, shame on *me!*" Do we really use conscientious, planned evaluation to maximize our dust and noise with very little lasting accomplishment?

I don't want to get to the end of my life and look back on nothing but "dust and noise." Yet so many people do. This is a big part of any midlife crisis. A person begins to realize that very little of their time has been spent accomplishing things that are truly of value. We need to evaluate our life's work as we go along.

Philosophy is supreme. You have to know God's purpose for you, for your ministry, and for the particular person or project you are evaluating. You must stay on target. A continual evaluation process has several benefits.

I. THE RIGHT COLABORERS

The right kind of colaborer is attracted to you and your ministry when you stay on track toward worthwhile goals. When you are helping people get worthwhile things done in a meaningful program, people want your leadership. Good evaluation of people and programs brings the right kind of team together.

2. COORDINATION OF EFFORTS

Constant evaluation also keeps that team working together. In evaluating the project and the people involved as the project develops, we avoid duplication—and conflicts—of efforts. It is far better to *avoid* hurt feelings and conflicts than it is to try to repair the damage later.

3. COVERAGE

We also see the areas being neglected. Evaluation is essential to the organization of the group effort in the cause of Christ.

4. COMMUNICATION OF PHILOSOPHY AND DIRECTION

This ongoing evaluation should be regularly communicated to the people who need to hear it. Some of it should be shared only with the individual to whom it pertains—especially if it is a reprimand or if it shows problems to work on. Some of it should be shared in staff meetings and preaching services. Freely discuss the changes in programs. This reaffirms the basic goals of the ministry and, at the same time, keeps everyone working together as the ministry grows and changes.

5. CONTINUATION

Evaluation brings out the best in people. "You don't get what you expect," the old saying goes, "but what you inspect." Unbalanced, this attitude could be cynical. Yet, all of us have two needs that are met by outside evaluation. First, we need a stimulus to keep on with the same enthusiasm with which we started. That is a part of the weakness of the flesh. Second, we need someone to help us see things that we overlook or misevaluate. That is why God stresses over and over again the need for counsel:

> Where no counsel is, the people fall: but in the multitude of counsellors is safety. (Proverbs 11:14)

> He that hearkeneth unto counsel is wise. (Proverbs 12:15)

> With the well-advised is wisdom. (Proverbs 13:10)

If you do not have someone evaluating you and your work, you need to seek out a source of honest counsel. One of the dangers in our independent, biblically-separated circles is the lack of accountability. The pastor, the school ad-

> **IF SOME OF US WENT OUT IN THE BUSINESS WORLD AND WORKED FOR A BOSS THE WAY WE WORK FOR THE LORD, WE WOULD BE FIRED IN A WEEK.**

ministrator, the missions director—those people at the top of some organizational chart—must actively seek out the honest input of others. If some of us went out in the business world and worked for a boss the way we work for the Lord, we would be fired in a week.

To avoid bitter disappointments at the end of life, we need to evaluate our programs, the people we are responsible for, and—most of all—our own progress toward lifetime goals.

TWO KINDS OF EVALUATION

Projects need evaluation as they are in process and after they are complete. The in-process evaluation is just part of leading. The "I

DO" method presented in Chapter 8 demands not only Initiation and Delegation, but also Oversight. Oversight is, by its nature, an ongoing evaluation.

I remember the time when a well-intentioned athletic director for our school ordered brand new basketball warm-ups, just like those worn by the Philadelphia 76ers. They were impressive looking and presented a great image, but it was done at the expense of $1,800. My lack of involvement and evaluation of this man's function led to his making a decision that he had no power to make.

Post-process evaluation is even more important. Yet this is the part that people most often skip. They are tired, they are busy, they are hurrying to the next task; essentially, they are creating so much noise and dust that they miss the still, small voice of the Lord. They do not see His warning signs.

In post-process evaluation you want to see what worked and what should be changed in the next similar project. The "Five Ws" make this analysis meaningful:

WHAT:	What was the event? What was the purpose of it? Was it achieved?
WHY:	Why did I have it? Why should I have it next time?
WHEN:	Was the timing right? When should we have it next time?
WHERE:	Where was it held? Is there a better place?
WHO:	Who was involved? Who else could have been involved?

Who could help lead this next time? Would someone who attended it this time be ready to lead it next time?

EVALUATING THE PROGRAM

The "dust and noise" at Tri-City settled down one day in 1976. In 1975, Tri-City had been recognized by a nationwide magazine as the fastest-growing church in Missouri. A banner, given as an award by that magazine, hung across the front of the auditorium. Early in 1976 we entered a major campaign. In one week we saw seven hundred professions of faith—a fantastic victory! Until we tried to follow up with those "converts." We saw very little genuine, lasting conversion.

Our goal was never to be a "fastest-growing church," or even a big church. We just wanted to fulfill the Great Commission. Our goal did not change, but we were shocked into evaluating our method. Were we using people to build a ministry? Or were we using a ministry to build people?

We began to build people. We became a family-oriented ministry. In the beginning the teens were mostly from lost homes, and I kept them busy most nights of the week. We had "Summer Sweep" and "Teenage Soulwinning" and "Marathon Saturdays," but they all emphasized the same thing: soulwinning. Now we began to say that church activities outside of the regular services would normally be on Saturday evenings. Christian school activities would be scheduled for Tuesday and Friday. With the Sunday and Wednesday evening church services included, this left at least Monday and Thursday reserved as family nights. We also stressed that the many activities of the church were designed to meet different needs and that not everyone is expected to be at everything planned.

However, we became a church of seminars. We taught series on the family and we went to Christian seminars. Our people learned and stabilized. Although we were still winning souls, the pendulum swung from evangelism to teaching. Unfortunately, we went too far in that direction. The sit-and-soak syndrome is at least as dangerous as the burnout program. After realizing this, we sought to attain a balance of evangelism and teaching.

> **THE GREAT COMMISSION IS A BALANCED PROGRAM.**

And that is what the Great Commission is. It is a balanced program. Read it again: "Go ye therefore, and teach all nations, baptizing them in the name of the Father, and of the Son, and of the Holy Ghost: Teaching them to observe all things whatsoever I have commanded you" (Matthew 28:19–20).

It could not be clearer. Verse 19 is a call to evangelism. We are to "make disciples" of all nations, presenting the message of salvation in Christ and leading them to the first act of obedience, baptism. But we cannot stop there. It is not enough to get them down the aisle and under the water.

In verse 20, we see that we need to teach those disciples to live the whole Christian life. Soulwinning is part of that. So are marital harmony, Christian childrearing, diligent and honest work, clearing one's conscience, and many other daily applications of Scripture.

As you evaluate your programs, you want to know more than simply whether they "worked" or not. You want to see if they worked together with the whole picture of what God has called you to do.

In evaluating church or school education, ask questions like these: Are the teachers being trained to communicate effectively in the classroom? Are students participating in class? Are Bibles being used effectively by teachers and students? Are teachers demonstrating Christian love and enthusiasm? Are curriculum materials thoroughly accurate and educationally sound? Are these materials being used to the best advantage by teachers and students?

In evaluating church records of evangelism and outreach, consider points like these: Are the various Sunday school classes showing numerical growth? Are people professing salvation through each outreach ministry? Where are these converts one year after baptism? Does the church pay as much attention to retaining people as it does to reaching new people?

These are just a few areas to consider, but every part of the ministry should pass through the fires of review. Evaluation takes work, but it saves the frustration of putting maximum effort into something that produces minimum results. If we expend many hours on projects that are not accomplishing God's goals for our ministries, what profit is that? Evaluation takes time, but it ultimately saves time.

EVALUATING THE PEOPLE

People naturally fear evaluation. We put on an appearance of confidence, but even the most confident and competent among us feel a little squeeze of anxiety at the thought of trusting our name and the evaluation of our work to someone else.

HELPING PEOPLE THROUGH EVALUATION

When you evaluate someone else, then, you must work to get past that person's uncertainty about your attitude, motives, and method. They should see the attitude of James 3:17: "*But the wisdom that is from above is first pure, then peaceable, gentle, and easy to be intreated, full of mercy and good fruits, without partiality, and without hypocrisy.*" What a list of qualities for the ministry leader! When you approach someone to discuss his or her role in the ministry, does that person go away saying that you were:

- *pure*—no hidden motives; up-front;
- *peaceable*—calm, resolving conflicts;
- *gentle*—you truly cared about their feelings;
- *easy to be entreated*—willing to listen;
- *full of mercy*—willing to give a second chance;
- *full of good fruits*—working at growing in your own ministry;
    - *without partiality*—not playing favorites; and
    - *without hypocrisy*—truly caring about their success within your ministry?

That is a pretty tough job description. But that is what it takes if you are going to maximize the benefits of the evaluation process. Your attitude is the key.

And your belief in your people is another key. Kenneth Blanchard and Spencer Johnson, in *The One Minute Manager*, put it this way:

Everyone is a potential winner.

Some people are disguised as losers.

Don't let their appearances fool you.[4]

When people know that you believe in them, they can more readily take criticism. This is an old saying, but it is true: "People don't care what you know, until they know that you care."

> WHEN PEOPLE KNOW THAT YOU BELIEVE IN THEM, THEY CAN MORE READILY TAKE CRITICISM.

Committed Christian workers want to grow. They want to do the Lord's work well. If you can—with gentleness and insight—help them to do that, they will generally appreciate your efforts.

HOW TO MAXIMIZE PERSONNEL EVALUATION

Let people know up-front what is expected of them. This is another benefit of having written job descriptions for the ministry, both for paid staff and volunteer layman positions. James Deuink and Carl Herbster state this in their book, *Effective Christian School Management*:

> In the typical Christian school the administrator is held ultimately accountable for everything that happens. The school board or pastor looks to the administrator to provide the professional and spiritual direction needed for the school's success. This expectation is quite reasonable. It is not reasonable, however, to fail to give the administrator sufficient direction for him to understand just what the

---

4   Kenneth Blanchard and Spencer Johnson, *The One Minute Manager* (New York: Morrow, 1982).

board's concept of successful operation is.[5]

From the first day on the job, if possible, let people know what is expected. Have clear, observable standards and periodic reviews so that people know what is expected.

Evaluations should be scheduled. Apart from "as needed" comments and help, everyone on staff should know when to expect a very positive evaluation conference—once a year is good for an experienced staff member. In the first year, once a quarter may be more appropriate. This gives a newcomer more of a chance to get off to the right start.

When you gather information for evaluations, be careful. Formal evaluations that request information from everyone in a group will give a more balanced view than unsolicited comments will. Acting on the comments of the vociferous minority hangs a sign on your office door: "Bring Gossip Here."

As I indicated before, these sessions should be positive. The sandwich approach is about as good as you can get. First, you praise. Say everything good that you can honestly say. Then you suggest areas of improvement. Finally, you conclude with positive statements again.

Do not forget to listen. An evaluation review should be a time for you, the leader, to learn some things, too. Are there ways that you can help this subordinate do a better job? Have you been the effective leader that he needed? How can your team function more effectively in the future? A meaningful evaluation session is a two-way street: a dialogue, not a diatribe.

---

5   James W. Deuink and Carl Herbster, *Effective Christian School Management* (Greenville, SC: Bob Jones University, 1986).

For the day-by-day, less detailed encounter, *The One Minute Manager* offers a powerful approach. Applying the one-minute praising to the ministry, you tell a person specifically what he did right. You tell him how good you feel about it and how it furthers the cause of Christ. You pause a moment to let him feel it with you. Then you encourage him to keep on. In the one-minute reprimand, similarly, you tell him specifically what he did wrong. Let him know how you feel about it and the problems that it caused. Then reaffirm that person's worth to yourself and to the ministry, and let that be the end of the matter.

How you help those under you do their job is a measure of your own success. You have been given the responsibility of helping others minister. Remember, "Whosoever will be chief among you, let him be your servant" (Matthew 20:27). One of your responsibilities as a servant, therefore, is to provide meaningful evaluation and help. You help others as you clearly, tactfully, and honestly tell them what they are doing right and what they are doing wrong. It is your responsibility to the individual and to the ministry. Olan Hendrix boldly states: "Occasionally you will meet a Christian worker who does not want to accomplish anything. Sometimes you will have to remove him from the pursuit of this goal and send him home. If one of these men embezzled $60, you would remove him. If he becomes involved in heresy, you ship him off. But he can wander around ineffectively on the field, and we do not do anything about it. I want to insist that it is not his fault. It is the top man's fault."[6]

Immediate evaluations—both praise and reprimand—are at least as important as the longer-range evaluations for helping people

---

6   Olan Hendrix, *Management for the Christian Leader* (Ada, MI: Baker, 1988).

grow in the ministry. But be careful of the timing in both. When someone is suffering under the weight of a major failure, that is not the time to twist the knife. Sometimes you do not have to reprimand, just help. When you cannot help, console. In this world of hurting people—pastors and parishioners alike—there is more need for encouragement than for scourging.

WHERE DID I PUT IT?

As important as the evaluation process is, it is critical that we keep accurate records, filed in a system that makes them readily available for the next time. Have you ever planned a picnic, a banquet, or an outing for your class and found yourself asking, "When we did this last year, what did we do about decorations? We ran short of punch last year; how much did we need? Do I still have the name of the person to call to reserve a shelter at the park?" Keeping meaningful records from one year to the next can save you hours of time.

I have found that a central filing system works best. When the annual church picnic is coming up, I ask the secretary to bring the file on the church picnic. I look at what was done last year, scan the evaluation sheet, and plan this year's picnic on the basis of those two things. I keep that file handy and continue to work on it through the organization and leading parts of the event. After the event is concluded, I write up my evaluation, put it back in the folder, and give it back to the secretary to return to the central file. This is a very simple but very effective system.

There is another benefit to the central file. When every staff member keeps his own records tucked away, you lose the program when you lose the person. The central file allows the ministry to learn and grow even as individuals may be called elsewhere.

THE MOST IMPORTANT EVALUATION

The beginning place for all evaluation is an honest, nothing-spared comparison of our activities with our life goals. What does it matter if we get a lot of things done, if those things do not contribute to the work God has called us to? In the rapid pace of the ministry, it is far too easy to get submerged in phone calls, urgent needs, and strident claims upon our time. The old book of wisdom, Proverbs, tells us to "ponder the path of [our] feet" (Proverbs 4:16).

THE GOOD VS. THE BEST

The good truly is the enemy of the best. We are to evaluate our life, we are to evaluate our family, and we are to evaluate our ministry to other people. Here is a simple three-step process for daily evaluation.

> **EVALUATION IS A CRITICAL PART OF OUR ONGOING MINISTRY.**

1. What **must** be done? This is the urgent. It must be done. There is no putting it off. It might be a message to prepare for tomorrow, a lesson to teach for today, or a project that is essential to complete. It could even be a person to encourage or a brother that must be confronted. Maybe it should have been done yesterday or even last week, but there is no putting it off now. I must get it done. This is the time to pray for God's direction and get it done. Maybe you wish you had more time for it, but you need to do all that you can to get it done now. Maybe it was given to you last minute and you might not even feel like doing it, but it must be done. This is where Colossians 3:22–23 comes in: "Do it heartily as to the Lord… knowing that from the Lord you shall receive the reward." I have had many of these situations over the years. Sometimes it was an

urgent matter coming up. Sometimes it was something I should have done before it became urgent. At other times, it was something handed to me at the last minute, but it still must be done.

2. What **needs** to be done? This is the important. Someone has said "the urgent is seldom important and the important is seldom urgent." Work on the important thing now before they become urgencies.

There are more options here. It is important and I need to be working on it now before it becomes an urgency. It could be working ahead of time on a message or a lesson. It might be a needy project to get done. The list is endless, but I need to be a wise steward and evaluate what priorities are important and need to get done now. This is where Colossians 3:24 reminds us that our service to the Lord will be rewarded by the Lord. These are sometimes things that we have planned and organized, or other jobs that have been assigned to us, but they are important and need to be done. We are to do our best for God and others.

3. What would I **like** to do? This involves many areas. It could be responsibilities that we have and we just want to get them done, or it may be things that we really look forward to doing and we have planned it in our schedules. The urgent and important areas are already taken care of and we want to get this done. This is where 1 Corinthians 10:31 applies: whatever we do should be for God's glory.

***

Life Principle:

Always be evaluating. Ephesians 5:15–17

FURTHER REFLECTIONS

The Annual Evaluation

Kevin Williams

Senior Pastor, Tri-City Baptist Church

Independence, Missouri

THE PRINCIPLES FOR FACILITATING REGULAR communication between staff members in this book are extremely important. In addition to weekly meetings and regular opportunities to cultivate relationships, an annual evaluation can be very helpful. This helps the leader and staff member to assess strengths and weaknesses in order to improve for the future.

At the end of the year (or school year), a meeting should be scheduled. Both parties should prepare for the meeting. The superior should evaluate the strengths and weaknesses of the one working under him. He should evaluate skills and character. A form with appropriate categories can be used in this process.

The staff member should review his job description and assign a percentage of his work week hours to each area. He should consider if he is operating within his areas of greatest skill. He should also be prepared to share constructive criticism with his superior. He should evaluate his own effectiveness and list things that he would like to see changed or added.

During the planned meeting, the superior should do all he can to encourage open communication and criticism. Rarely will a staff member voluntarily criticize his leader if he does not ask for it. Sadly, the staff may criticize and complain to others without ever sharing their concerns with the one who can do something about it. This, of course, is ungodly, but the leader should take the initiative to ask for criticism.

This meeting can be a great time for both parties to express appreciation for each other. The superior may need to address a weakness, but he should seek to offer praise as well. Good workers look forward to opportunities for feedback. They want to know what they are doing well, and they want to improve wherever is necessary.

Annual evaluations can be used in many different areas of ministry. The pastor can meet with his assistant pastors. The deacons could evaluate the pastor and meet with him. The school principal can meet with each teacher. This can even be done with lay workers in the church. The pastor can meet with those who oversee outreach, children, facility, etc. The youth pastor can get feedback from parents.

It is not rare that people get frustrated in ministry. They wonder if they are doing a good job. They feel they are not appreciated. They may lack proper training and direction. They are worn out. They feel overwhelmed. Without communication about these things, good workers will eventually quit or leave. It is the leader's responsibility to encourage and equip those in his oversight. He must praise their strengths and help with weaknesses.

Regular communication is vital for effective ministry. We labor together for the cause of Christ. Working in unity requires communication. The annual evaluation can be a great tool to help a ministry continue to serve the Lord in unity. It will help God's servants evaluate the past and become more effective in the future.

CHAPTER 10

THE CALL TO PROPER USE OF TIME

For a thousand years in the sight are but as yesterday when it is past,

and as a watch in the night. So teach us to number our days, that we

may

apply our hearts unto wisdom.

Psalm 90:4, 12

And if ye call on the Father, who without respect of persons

judgeth according to every man's work,

pass the time of your sojourning here in fear.

1 Peter 1:17

HOW OFTEN HAVE YOU HEARD or said things like this:

" I'd spend more time in God's Word if I only had the time."

"With more time, I could be involved in discipleship."

"I would spend more time preparing for my classes, but I stay so busy!"

Everyone has the same twenty-four hours in a day, the same one hundred sixty-eight hours in a week. Why is it that some people seem to get more accomplished in those hours than others do? Some of this difference is related to gifts and abilities, true. However, there is a more powerful factor than that. Some people *plan* on getting more done and, as a result, they *do* get more accomplished.

Time is a precious commodity. "It's just a minute, but eternity is in it." The minutes that we have to spend here will bring lasting satisfaction both here and hereafter if we invest them wisely.

We live in a fast-paced society. A continual series of demands pounds at our lives like waves crashing against a shore. I remember looking at some faculty members at three o'clock in the afternoon. They looked like they had been through World War III—and lost. Then, they remember—tonight is midweek service! Isn't that great! They would get to go home, grade papers, prepare for tomorrow, and be back by seven o'clock for church! And they got tired.

If your church is like the ones I've served in, you have programs that could keep you going twenty-four hours a day, eight days a week! I can get tired just thinking of all the programs, but each of them is designed to help people accomplish one of the priorities of life. Yet that does not mean that I need to be involved in every one of these programs: I probably should not be. (However, some things are indispensable for the meeting of our own needs and for our testimony. Among these indispensables, I include the regular services of the church and special series such as revivals, evangelistic meetings, and missionary conferences.) All of us must study how we can have the right kind of relationships with the people and still handle the responsibilities God has brought into our lives. It comes down to using our time properly.

PLAN YOUR WORK DAILY

In my ministry, I have found that a key to time management is advance planning. The interesting thing is that I learned this principle a long time before entering the ministry. In the business world I used to set goals all the time. I used to plan my day every day. Somehow, though, it took me a long time to realize that I should approach the ministry the same way.

If you are a schoolteacher, have you ever wondered who came up with the idea of lesson plans? I'm sure you'd like to catch that person! Still, that person did us a favor. Lesson plans are just a reflection of the type of man-

> "THE IMPORTANT THINGS ARE SELDOM URGENT, AND THE URGENT THINGS ARE SELDOM IMPORTANT." – PRESIDENT EISENHOWER

agement skill that executives spend hundreds of dollars to learn at seminars. They are just tools to help us accomplish what we want to do that day.

President Eisenhower said, "The important things are seldom urgent, and the urgent things are seldom important." Yet, we find ourselves so often doing the urgent. The principal expects the report at three o'clock. At ten minutes to three you are feverishly working away. Why? It has become urgent. You are supposed to have a program plan ready for one of your nineteen church committees, and you are writing while you are driving to church. Why? Urgency triumphs again. If you will plan every day in terms of three levels of tasks, you will get more done, you will get it done better, and you will enjoy doing it more.

First, plan the urgent things. These must be done today. Second, plan the important things. They are not urgent yet, but they relate to upcoming projects. They must be done sooner or later; and the sooner they are done, the better off you are so that a crisis does not arise. You will find that you can do a much better job before the crisis comes. Third, write down one or two things you would like to do. These might be tasks as small as cleaning out a file folder or a drawer.

We usually accomplish two out of these three categories. We address the urgencies because we have to. We usually find time for some of the projects we like to do. The items in the middle category, the important things, are the ones neglected.

Take about twenty minutes either in the morning or in the evening to plan your day. Personally, I like to do it at the beginning of the day. I have discovered that after 8:00 a.m. it is hard to do that planning at our ministry. There is always activity and interruption.. Being an early riser, I have found that I can get more done between 6:00 a.m. and 8:00 a.m. than I can from 8:00 a.m. to 6:00 p.m. when the business of dealing with people, meetings, and crises overtake my list of tasks. If I am going to plan my day, I have to do it long before 8:00 a.m.

There are various forms that you can use. You will find readymade forms at office supply stores; you can copy forms included in the appendix; you can draw up your own; and you can find just about any form for any purpose on the internet. Just do it. At the beginning of the day or at the end, in preparation for tomorrow, sort through your papers and write a priority list—a *To Do* list.

I find that when working from such a list, I get more accomplished than on days that I just begin work without planning ahead.

Much more significant work is done, and I have a real feeling of accomplishment because I know that the important things have been done.

WORK YOUR PLAN DAILY

Plan your work and work your plan! Someone once said, "In order to be successful, three things must be done. First, you must set goals. Second, you must work toward these goals. Third, they

> **PLAN YOUR WORK AND WORK YOUR PLAN!**

must be worthwhile goals." Many times we set goals, and we sincerely intend to work toward them. However, we never get around to them.

Two fellow students at my college made a big impression on me. They are probably still there today. One was John; I called him "Test." Every time I talked to him he was having a test the next day.

"How are you doing, John?"

"Oh, boy, I tell you what. I've got a test tomorrow. Man, I'm worried about it."

"Test" was there when I came, and he was there when I left. For four years he was having tests all the time. Most of the time it was the same classes, same tests, over and over. He was concerned, but he wasn't taking much productive action.

The other was Rich. We called him "All-nighter." His characteristic statement was, "Hey, you want to pull an all-nighter with me? Boy, I've got a big test tomorrow, and I'm going to pull an all-nighter. You want to do that with me?"

Okay, I pulled a couple of all-nighters with Rich. About dinnertime he would ask, "Hey, you gonna pull that all-nighter with me?"

"Yeah, I'll do it with you."

About 10:30 p.m. we'd sit down with our books. He would look at a page for a few minutes, and then he would get a brainstorm.

"You hungry?"

"Yeah, I'm a little hungry."

"Well, let's go out and get a burger."

So we would drive to an all-night hamburger stand. All the way out and all the way back, Rich would talk about the all-nighter we were going to pull. We would get back, sit down, and study for a few minutes. They Rich would say, "Man, how about some popcorn? Don't you want some popcorn? "

So we would get out the popcorn popper and get that going. At about 2:30 a.m. we had the popcorn ready, and we would sit down at the books again. We were still on the same page as at 10:30. After

> **DO NOT WASTE SO MUCH TIME MAKING THE PERFECT PLAN THAT YOU NEVER IMPLEMENT ANY PLAN.**

a while he would say, "Boy, I am tired! If I go to bed and get an hour's rest, I'll be a lot fresher in the morning." So All-nighter would get his hour's rest, which usually lasted the remainder of the night. He would get up in the morning unprepared and fail his test.

Rich had goals and good intentions. He meant to do well in school, but he did not follow through.

The moral of the story is this: Do it! Your plan does not have to be perfect. Do not waste so much time making the perfect plan that you never implement any plan.

There will always be interruptions. Telephone calls and walk-in visitors need attention. I also realize that some people have a more flexible schedule than others. If you are scheduled to teach from 8:00 a.m. to 3:00 p.m. and then to coach a team after that, you cannot just pick your time of day to work on projects. In either case, the daily *To Do* list is your most valuable time-management tool.

Psychologically, what happens is this: that list in front of you keeps you on target. When you have that open ten or thirty minutes in the day, you do not have to decide what to do. It is right there in front of you. When you have a list of jobs in front of you, it will cause you to shorten a phone call, to spend less time in idle conversation with someone, or limit your time on the computer. You find more efficient ways to do things. Instead of darting down the hall for a one-minute conference, which often turns out to be thirty minutes, you write a note.

Communicating in writing will many times reduce the misunderstandings that often result from verbal communication. Be careful in this, though. Exclamation points and question marks can be taken as hostile or pointed criticism unless the context is clearly positive. However, verbal communication is sometimes the best method. This is especially true if you are dealing with a problem. People can read into a written communication something that you did not intend.

Fastest is not always best; but in any situation, keep in front of you the jobs on your *To Do* list. A plan is not any good if we do not use it. Plan your work and work your plan.

WORK IN TIME BLOCKS

A time block, no matter how long, is a time set aside to do one particular task or a group of related tasks. Answer all of your e-mails at one time. Return your phone calls in another time block. If you have ten minutes before you have to go to a meeting, that can be a time block to knock out a couple of e-mails. You might also have a particular time each day when you are scheduled to make phone calls. I usually do that between 9:00 and 10:00 a.m. Try to group your meetings, errands, visits, etc., for maximum efficiency. One of my pet peeves is to come home from the church and then find out that I need to go back to the store that I just passed to get some small item.

Interruptions will come, and I am not saying that we should not be flexible. If you have a Philippian jailer fall on his knees in your office and ask, "What must I do to be saved?" you cannot say, "Come back Thursday night at 7:00. That's my soulwinning time." Just realize

> IF YOU MUST LEAVE A TASK, GET BACK TO IT PROMPTLY OR RESCHEDULE IT FOR ANOTHER SUITABLE TIME SOON.

that flexible things bend both ways. If you must leave a task, get back to it promptly or reschedule it for another suitable time *soon*.

Even family time needs to be blocked-in. When my kids were young, we tried to keep Monday and Thursday nights free of church or school activities. I tried to keep Thursday night free for Family Night at our house. We worked to get the homework and chores out of the way early and just have a good time together. Because family is important, the Family Night rates a regularly scheduled time block. If someone asked me to do something on Thursday night, I would tell him that I already had a commitment. I did not always do that; I had to learn the hard way. However, my family has always been one of my top priorities. I wanted to lock in prime time for them, rather than give them the leftovers of my schedule.

PREPARE A TIMETABLE FOR COMPLETING BIG PROJECTS

Sometimes a large project can be downright intimidating. When you divide it into a number of sequential, smaller projects and put them on the calendar, it may not seem so hard to get started after all.

Personally, I hate to paint a room. I do not mind the actual painting; it is the preparation and cleanup that I have a hard time with. I have found that the project is not so bad when I have a timetable for completion. One night I take an hour to gather the materials. The next night I apply the masking tape. Then on Saturday morning I am all set to paint. But if I get up on Saturday morning and think of having to get the paint, find the tools and supplies, move furniture, and tape the walls, it sounds as if it will take forever.

It helps to break a large goal down into smaller segments. On big projects this is imperative.

ELIMINATE TIME WASTERS

If you have been a schoolteacher for any length of time, I hope you have come up with a set of procedures to streamline routine activities. After having papers come in every which way and then spending hours of the week, in total, alphabetizing them, teachers find better ways. They might have the students sit alphabetically; or they might have papers come in by rows, regardless of alphabetization, and then pass them back by rows the next day.

A staff member I knew some years ago wrestled with a different time waster. He was a truly excellent Sunday school teacher, but every Sunday morning about 6:00 a.m. you would find him in the church office pecking out his outline on a typewriter. This was not a "Saturday night special." I believe he had been preparing all week, but he had gotten into the habit of preparing his outline, running off copies, and making an overhead transparency on Sunday morning. It would take him until about 8:00 or 8:15. I challenged him to prepare the outline earlier in the week. We had secretaries who would be glad to do the work that he was doing on Sunday morning—and they could do it much faster, too! If he could prepare a handwritten draft of his outline by Friday morning, a secretary would type it and make copies for Sunday. This would save him about an hour and a half each week.

Granted, not everyone has a secretary waiting to help out. Still, each of us needs to find the quickest ways of accomplishing things. We need to spend our time deliberately. Let's look at some typical time traps.

The first is taking on someone else's task. Two teachers might be standing in the hall after school talking about the volleyball team and how they would run it if they were in charge. That is really none of their business unless they really intend to provide some positive input to the coach. We often waste our time talking about someone else's ministry. It is good to discuss a problem and come up with solutions if you are part of the solution. If you are not, then you need to either stay out of it or go to someone who is part of the solution.

The next time waster is unannounced visitors. You have your *To Do* list on your desk, and you are working away. Then someone walks in and asks, "You got a minute?" Have you ever known one of those conversations to stop at the one-minute mark? Do not be afraid to let people know that you are working on a project. Give your visitor a specific time when you can stop and talk, and write that into your day's plan. Of course, be balanced. Do not be abrupt. Express concern to meet that person's need. But stay on target as much as possible.

Lengthy telephone conversations are a problem, too. Do not spend thirty minutes saying what could be said in two. After your next lengthy phone call, think back on

> **THE LORD JESUS . . . SPENT MUCH OF HIS TIME TRAINING OTHERS TO MEET NEEDS.**

the information that you really needed to get or to give. Was the length of the phone call justifiable? Or did you spend a lot of time in idle conversation? Even in difficult situations, with someone grieving or in the hospital, we can show concern; and there is a time for just spending time with someone. But do it deliberately. Be sure your schedule isn't so crowded that there is no room for people.

Overcommitment is another time waster. Sometimes you just have to say no. When I was an associate pastor, I was involved in most of the ministries that involved lay people. It never bothered me for someone to say no (and it still doesn't). If someone told me that he did not believe that he should take on another responsibility because he had too many things going, that would not bother me in the least. I once believed that a need constituted a call. If I saw a need, then I thought I was called to meet that particular need. I found out that I could not meet all of the needs.

The Lord Jesus met needs, but He did not meet all of the needs. Rather, He spent much of His time training others to meet needs. Knowing that His earthly ministry would be short, He spent much time in discipleship. So we must train others to do what we do.

In too many ministries, we have too few people doing too much. Ninety percent of the work is done by ten percent of the people. In any ministry, a practical goal should be to have everybody involved in doing something appropriate to their gifts and spiritual maturity. Sometimes it is inviting people into their homes. Sometimes it is teaching Sunday school or being a class helper. Sometimes it is discipleship or the bus ministry. But there is something for anyone who is willing to get involved. Yet, we must be careful that we do not get people overcommitted. We must be conscious of their time and of their other responsibilities.

Unnecessary or poorly planned meetings are big time-wasters. First, is the meeting really necessary? I believe in communication: it is an essential for effective ministry. However, could this be communicated in another way? A meeting is not needed for everything. If a meeting is the way to go, then start with a list of topics, start on time, and have a proposed ending time. Do not wait for stragglers. Show your consideration for the time of those who are present by starting on time. Then make the meeting productive. Lengthy discussions that result in merely tabling a matter for later discussion are fruitless.

Finally, do not let recurring crises waste time. Set up reminder systems, such as a tickler file. In the tickler file, there is a file folder for each month. If the buses are due to be inspected in June, make note of the maintenance check that must be done and put the note in the May folder. Such notes, then, are translated into *To Do* lists at the start of each month.

CHECKLIST FOR GETTING MORE DONE

Let's summarize ten keys for getting more done:

- Always work with a *To Do* list
- Assign priorities and work accordingly
- Plan every day before you get into action
- Delegate whenever possible
- Try to work by time blocks
- Avoid or control interruptions
- Avoid overcommitment by learning to say no
- Divide big tasks into small segments
- Don't be afraid to ask for help
- Set up reminder systems

Managing your time is managing yourself. Sloppy time management is caused by bad habits and a lack of organizational skills. It is really a lack of self-discipline. It results in frustration, inefficiency, tiredness, and burnout. Time is a precious commodity. Recognizing our responsibility to use it wisely will help us overcome time-management problems. God has given each of us enough time to do what He wants us to do, if we do not waste our time.

***

Life Principle:
Prioritize your time for maximum effectiveness. Eph 5:14-16

FURTHER REFLECTIONS

TIME MANAGEMENT

TIME MANAGEMENT IS STEWARDSHIP: STEWARDSHIP of self, stewardship of our time, and stewardship of our money. Let's consider the element of time in assessing the power of getting things done. Let's take a further look at those ten keys of getting more things done listed in the chapter. A good overview passage is Ephesians 5:15–16, "See then that you walk circumspectly, not as fools, but as wise, redeeming the time because the days are evil."

1. Always work with a *To Do* list. It has been several years since the first writing of this book. That has been mentioned, but I must emphasize again the importance of a *To Do* list. There have been many days over the years that I have used a written *To Do* list, as well as many days that I have not. In both situations I have stayed very busy, but the key to getting the important things done before they become a frustrating urgency is having a list of what needs to be done and working from that list. Working from a *To Do* list also saves me from embarrassing moments of forgetting important things. It can be a written *To Do* list, an electronic one, fancy or simple, but most importantly—a *To Do* list is a must for effectiveness.

2. Assign priorities and work accordingly. It is one thing to have a *To Do* list, but another to label the priorities and begin to work from it. May I say one last time, "plan your work and then work your plan" for maximum effectiveness: Ephesians 5:16, "redeeming the time."

3. Plan every day before you get into action. Years ago when I was in the business world, a wise district manager taught me what he called the most important twenty minutes of the day. He challenged me to take twenty minutes either at the beginning of the day or at the end of the day to plan what was needed to do before I got into the busy activity of that day. He was right. I've learned since then that the time with the Word is most important, but next to it this twenty minutes is key to successful ministry.

4. Delegate whenever possible. Delegation has been discussed earlier. We cannot always delegate, but I have found that it can be done more than we sometimes want to admit. Review chapter 2 and 7 concerning maximum effectiveness. Wise delegation is a blessing to the delegator, to the one delegated to, and the ministry over all.

5. Try to work in time blocks. Working in time blocks allows us to take large projects and break them down to accomplish goals. Try putting e-mails and phone calls into time segments.

6. Avoid or control interruptions. Interruptions do occur and we are to be servants of the people, but notice the statement: avoid interruptions and control interruptions. I try to control where and when I work and study, so that I can maximize my time effectiveness. Evaluate your time effectiveness for yourself.

7. Avoid overcommitment by learning to say no. Evaluate continually; get input from your spouse, family, superior, and co-workers to avoid overcommitment. The good can

be an enemy of the best here.

8. Divide big tasks into small segments. Begin your planning in advance for large projects. How can you break it down into small segments along the way?

9. Don't be afraid to ask for help. There are people who are more gifted in certain areas than we are. Ask for their help by trading gifts, abilities, and projects. Be a blessing to one another.

10. Set up reminder systems to get things done. There are many reminder systems out there. Use what is available and effective to remind you. Whatever you set up, just use it. Personally, I like having to write down on a separate list what I haven't yet accomplished: this forces me to be reminded along the way.

APPENDIX

POLICY MANUAL TABLE OF CONTENTS

TABLE OF CONTENTS

PERSONAL PLANNING SHEET

NAME: _____

Year: _____

SPIRITUAL GOALS:				
FAMILY GOALS:				
PHYSICAL GOALS:				
MENTAL GOALS:				
FINANCIAL GOALS:				
SOCIAL GOALS:				

WEEKLY PLANNER

Goals for the Week	Needs to Perform		
1.	a.		
	b.		
	c.		
2.	a.		
	b.		
	c.		
3.	a.		
	b.		
	c.		
4.	a.		
	b.		
	c.		
5.	a.		
	b.		
	c.		
6.	a.		
	b.		
	c.		
7.	a.		
	b.		
	c.		
8.	a.		
	b.		
	c.		
9.	a.		
	b.		
	c.		
10.	a.		
	b.		
	c.		
Write	Visit	Call	Personal

THINGS I MUST DO	THINGS THAT I WOULD LIKE TO ACCOMPLISH

THINGS TO DO *today* . . .

Date _____

1. _____

2. _____

3. _____

4. _____

5. _____

6. _____

7. _____

8. _____

9. _____

10. _____

11. _____

12. _____

13. _____

14. _____

15. _____

16. _____

"Redeeming the time, because the days are evil" (Ephesians 5:16).

DAILY PLANNER

Date _____

THINGS TO DO TODAY

_____ _____
_____ _____
_____ _____
_____ _____
_____ _____
_____ _____
_____ _____
_____ _____
_____ _____
_____ _____

7:00 _____   1:30 _____
7:30 _____   2:00 _____
8:00 _____   2:30 _____
8:30 _____   3:00 _____
9:00 _____   3:30 _____
9:30 _____   4:00 _____
10:00 _____   4:30 _____
10:30 _____   5:00 _____
11:00 _____   5:30 _____
11:30 _____   6:00 _____
12:00 _____   6:30 _____
12:30 _____   7:00 _____
1:00 _____   7:30 _____

TIME INVENTORY SHEET FOR USE IN IDENTIFYING TIME ROBBERS

What I Plan to Do Tomorrow   What I Actually Did

_____ 8:00 _____
_____ 8:30 _____
_____ 9:00 _____
_____ 9:30 _____
_____ 10:00 _____
_____ 10:30 _____
_____ 11:00 _____
_____ 11:30 _____
_____ 12:00 _____
_____ 12:30 _____
_____ 1:00 _____
_____ 1:30 _____
_____ 2:00 _____
_____ 2:30 _____
_____ 3:00 _____
_____ 3:30 _____
_____ 4:00 _____
_____ 4:30 _____
_____ 5:00 _____

How much time was used as scheduled? _____ Unscheduled? _____

What were the time robbers that got me off schedule? _____

_____

_____

For more information about
Matt Williams
&
HOW TO BE TEAM PLAYER
AND ENJOY IT
please visit:

Website: www.tri-city.org
Email: mwilliams@tri-city.org

....

For more information about
AMBASSADOR INTERNATIONAL
please visit:

www.ambassador-international.com
@AmbassadorIntl
www.facebook.com/AmbassadorIntl

www.ingramcontent.com/pod-product-compliance
Lightning Source LLC
LaVergne TN
LVHW051550080426
835510LV00020B/2939